LEARN JAPANESE

Get the Basics, Vacation with Ease, Start Conversations, and Sound Fluent When You're Not

RIN KIMOTO

TABLE OF CONTENTS

INTRODUCTION

So you want to learn the Japanese language, but you can't figure out where you should start. Perhaps you're planning a vacation to Japan, and just want to get around effortlessly without getting overwhelmed?

Or maybe you want to integrate a bit more into the language without sticking out as a regular tourist, and sound more fluent?

That's what this book is here to do, clearly and concisely. The only cost you will face is the cost of this book and nothing else. You can study and learn at your own pace and in whatever way works best for you. You'll also find that everything is structured in a way that makes sense and naturally progresses from the alphabets to simple sentences.

I'll be honest with you, this book won't make you fluent in Japanese overnight, but what it can do is have you speaking Japanese in a couple of hours. You'll know how to say simple things, ask simple questions, and you'll have an excellent understanding of the two main Japanese alphabets.

Japanese is not only a new language to learn, but it is also a beautiful language.

Chapter 1

THE DIFFICULTIES AHEAD

It seems the Japanese language has its own little family in the language world, although there are some linguists who believe it could be related to Turkish and Korean. Japanese is spoken as the mother tongue by the 130 million people who live in Japan, as well as the expatriates all over the world.

There are quite a few differences between English and Japanese, the big one being sentence structure, which tends to make it hard for most English-speaking people to learn Japanese at the same rate that they would learn Spanish or French.

The alphabet is also another big difference. The Japanese have a very complex writing system. There are three main scripts; one is known as the kanji, which is a group of characters with Chinese origins. The other two are hiragana and katakana. Modern Japanese will also make use of the Latin script in advertising. In this book, we will be focusing on what is known as the kana, which is made up of the hiragana and katakana.

Japanese is normally writing in columns from top to bottom and right to left. Japanese books start "at the back." In modern times, the Japanese language is printed or written in the same order of words that the English language is.

The next big difference is phonology. In Japanese, there are five pure vowel sounds that can be long or short. The syllable structure is very simple, typically, with the vowel sound being preceded by one of 15 consonant sounds. There are few complex consonant sounds, like with the words Christmas and strength in the English language. This means pronouncing Japanese words tends to be a lot easier than pronunciations in English.

Intonations between the Japanese and English languages don't have many commonalities, either. Some of the meanings that English speakers will convey by stress or change of pitch are a lot different than how they would be expressed in Japanese. This is where the practice is very important, as well as watching videos of native speakers.

Another big difference is with grammar, specifically, verb and tense. In Japanese, voice and tense are conveyed through changes to the verb form, just like in English. The difference is that the Japanese language doesn't have auxiliary verbs. Verbs in Japanese don't change, depending on the number or person. This means verbs in Japanese may actually be easier to learn than English, but it could also mean that they may be slightly more confusing.

Another difference in Japanese grammar is the subject-object-verb word order. Prepositions come after the noun, and the subordination conjunctions come after their clause. Other particles will come after the sentence. Adjectival phrases will always come before the noun they modify. Articles aren't a part of the Japanese language.

The good news is there are a large number of English words that are also used in Japanese. This could help you when you begin studying. Sometimes, though, the biggest challenge people have in learning Japanese, and this is true for the other way around as well, is the difference in the cultures. Communication between Japanese people is largely influenced by things like relative status, relationship, age, and sex. The Japanese will often avoid embarrassing themselves and the person they are talking to. So, when you have your first conversation with a native Japanese speaker, don't be surprised if it feels very different from the conversations you have in English.

The last thing I will advise you before we leave this chapter is to read things out loud. When it comes to learning how to pronounce things in Japanese, the best way to learn is to hear it. So don't be afraid to start saying the forthcoming sentences out loud so that you can get a feel for it.

Chapter 2

LEARNING THE KANA

Japanese has three scripts, or you could call them alphabets, called the katakana, hiragana, and kanji.

The kanji is made up of Chinese characters that have been adopted by modern Japanese writings. The majority of Japanese words are written using kanji. In Japanese, no spaces are used, so kanji helps to show you where a new word begins. Simply put, kanji is a symbol that represents words. The kanji could be looked at like an emoji. The more you start learning the kanji, the easier you may find it to read Japanese. However, we are going to learn how to read Japanese without learning about the kanji characters.

We are going to be focusing on the katakana and hiragana, which is collectively referred to as the kana.

There is a very good reason for doing this. Katakana and hiragana are made up of a little less than 50 characters each. While this may seem like a lot, if you stop and think about it, you have uppercase lowercase and cursive letters in English, and that comes out to about 104 different appearances.

Every single one of the katakana and hiragana characters makes its own phonetic sounds, just like with the English alphabet. You say "ko" when you see the character こ. The sound of "n" is represented by ン. The "ni" sound is に. While the "chi" sound is ち. And "wa" is shown as わ. When you put all of this together, you get "Konnichiwa"or こんにちわ. Pretty easy, right? The hiragana can be used to read the sounds in kanji characters.

Katakana and hiragana will use the same sounds, but they will use different characters. You can see the differences in the following charts.

HIRAGANA

Hiragana (ひらかな) is typically used for grammar. Remember when I was talking about the emojis? If you were to draw a star and then write "ing" after it, it would be read as staring. When it comes to Japanese, the "ing" would be expressed in hiragana. Participles, expressions, and words that have difficult-to-read or rare kanji characters tend to be written mainly in hiragana. Hiragana is often easier to spot since it is often simpler and curvier than the kanji form.

日本語額しいおめでとございます

You will notice that certain Japanese words will use more hiragana than kanji, like with kawaii (かわいい) or sayonara (さようなら).

Hiragana Chart

•	w	r	y	m	h	n	t	s	k	
ん n/m	わ wa	ら ra	や ya	ま ma	は ha	な na	た ta	さ sa	か ka	あ a
		り ri		み mi	ひ hi	に ni	ち chi	し shi	き ki	い i
		る ru	ゆ yu	む mu	ふ fu	ぬ nu	つ tsu	す su	く ku	う u
		れ re		め me	へ he	ね ne	て te	せ se	け ke	え e
	を o	ろ ro	よ yo	も mo	ほ ho	の no	と to	そ so	こ ko	お o

Learning hiragana will create a foundation for learning Japanese. Hiragana will give you the basic pronunciations in Japanese. It will also give you more resources for learning Japanese. All of the best Japanese learning tools will require you to know hiragana. Basically, this is the first step you need to take.

There are a lot of classes that will make you learn hiragana over several months. This isn't necessary. Learning hiragana should only take you a few days, maybe a week. You may even find that you can learn it in only a few hours. How long it will take you to learn will all depend on you, but the steps that follow should have you learning hiragana quickly.

There are some things we are going to implement during the learning process:

1. Mnemonics – Since it is relatively simple, at least, when you compare it to kanji, image-based mnemonics will help you to memorize things. I will give you an image with each character that should help you to remember it.

2. No writing (at least at first) – I know this sounds crazy, but when did you last write

something by hand? Most of our communication nowadays is spoken or typed. Trying to learn to write this out by hand will double or triple your learning speed. You can start learning this after you already understand them.

3. Exercises – There will be exercises that will help you to memorize hiragana. When you are performing these exercises, you need to make yourself recall the items, even if you think you won't be able to figure out the answer. The more effort you put into trying to recall something, the stronger the memory becomes.

Before you can actually memorize hiragana, you have to know how to pronounce everything. To start, we need to learn the vowels. The pronunciation of a/i/u/e/o is the most important, and all the other pronunciations are a combination of those letters, along with a consonant. That means the same basic sounds will simply be used. Let's get started then.

• あいうえお a-i-u-e-o

A あ: this is pronounced like "a" in words like father or car. To help you remember the shape

11

of the kana, try to spot the capital "A" within it. When you see this capital "A," you will know that it is "a," which is あ.

I い: this is pronounced like the "ee" in the word eel. To help you recall this kana, try thinking about two eels.

U う: this is pronounced like the "ou" in the word you or the "oo" in the word book. In order to remember this kana, look at its "U" shape. While it may be sideways, it is still easy to see.

E え: this is said like "e" in egg or exotic. To help you recall the shape of this kana, try picturing the shape of an exotic bird. The fancy feathers on the top of its head tell you that this isn't some normal bird but an exotic bird. Birds also lay eggs.

O お: this is pronounced like "oh." When you look at this kana, you can see that there are two Os in it. This one is easy to mix up with あ. Once you have figured out how to differentiate the two kanas, then you shouldn't have any problems. If you remember to look for the "A" in **あ** and the "oo" in the **お**, then you should be good to go.

- **かきくけこ** ka-ki-ku-ke-ko

The next column is the "k-column" of hiragana. This means you will add a "k" sound to the vowels you have already learned. This means you will have ka-ki-ku-ke-ko. This column doesn't have any weird exceptions like some of the others.

KA **か**: this is pronounced like the **あ** with a k sound in front of it. To remember this kana, think of a can-can dancer. It helps you remember the kana, as well as the pronunciation of it.

KI **き**: this is pronounced like the **い** with a k sound in front of it. In fact, all you have to do is remember the word "key." The kana not only looks like a key, but it is pronounced that way as well.

KU く: this is pronounced like the う with a k sound in front of it. Think about a cuckoo clock. To remember the kana, think about the beak on a little bird screaming coo-coo!

KE け: this pronounced like the え with a k sound in front of it. This would be the "ke" sound in the word "keg." You could use your imagination with that, as well, to remember this kana. It looks similar to a keg if you squint your eyes.

KO こ: this is pronounced like the お with a k sound in front of it. This is said like the "co" in cohabitation. You can recall this kana by picturing a couple of (co)rds lying next to each other.

• さしすせそ sa-shi-su-se-so

The "s-column" is the next column to learn. You will learn your first exception in this column, and that would be the "si," which, as you can see, is really "shi." It's said as "she" and won't stick to the same patterns that we have learned so far.

SA さ: like in the k column, you simply add an s sound before the あ. You can think about this kana as a weird sign stuck in the ground. The "si" in "sign" makes the "sa" sound, so focus more on the pronunciation of it and not the spelling when thinking about this mnemonic.

SHI し: we've covered this one already, but it is pronounced "she." Remember, this is the first kana that doesn't follow the other patterns we have seen, but this won't be the last exception.

SU す: this is pronounced like "sue." To remember the kana, think about a (su)wing swinging around throwing a little kid off of it.

SE せ: this is pronounced like the "se" in sexy. When you think about this kana, think about a man's smile with a large tooth in it. What is that person going to say (se)?

SO そ: this is pronounced just as it is spelled, "so." To remember this kana, think about a (so)ngbird flapping its wings.

• たちつてと ta-chi-tsu-te-to

Moving on to the next column, we have the "t-column." You've had to remember a lot of things so far, and there is more to come. Hopefully, the mnemonics are helping you out. There will be an exception in this column, just like the last. In fact, there are two.

TA た: this is pronounced like "ta" as in "ta-da." Remembering the kana for this one should be easy because it looks a lot like ta.

CHI ち: this is exception number one in this column but the second exception overall. This is not a "ti" sound, but a "chi" sound, as in energy. If you look at the kana, it looks like the profile of a face. To remember the kana and sound, think of a (chi)n on a person's face.

TSU つ: another exception and is pronounced just like "tsu." Again, there isn't a "tu." Instead, it is "tsu."

TE て: this is pronounced like the "te" in "ten." This kana looks like an uppercase "T."

TO と: this is pronounced like the "to" in "toe." You can remember the kana by thinking about a little toe with a splinter or nail in it.

• なにぬねの na-ni-nu-ne-no and はひふへほ ha-hi-hu/fu-he-ho

This group is bigger than the rest of them. There will be ten things in this group, but don't worry. You are getting better the further you go along.

NA な : this is said like the "na" in banana. To help recall this kana, try thinking about a naughty nun praying in front of a cross. The cross in the air should be the biggest giveaway for this kana.

NI に: this is said like the "nee" in a needle. To aid in the recall of this kana, try thinking about a needle pulling the thread.

NU ぬ : this is pronounced like the "noo" in noodles. There are many other kanas that look like ぬ, but you can recognize this one as noodles because there aren't any sharp sides. This one is completely bendable and smooth, just like noodles.

NE ね: this is pronounced like the "ne" in Nelly. Think about a cat to remember this kana. This is "Nelly the cat." There are similar-looking kana, but you will know this one because there is a loop at the end, and that's for Nelly's tail.

NO の: this one is pronounced just like the word "no." To recall this one, you could think about a "no smoking" sign.

HA は: this one sounds just like "ha." This kana looks similar to an uppercase "H" as well as the lowercase "a."

HI ひ: this is pronounced like "he." If you look at the kana, it looks like an up-close view of a big nose and two eyes. Think about how he (hi) has a big nose.

FU/HU ふ: this is typically pronounced with the f and not the h, so it sounds (fu)reaky, but it also resembles a hula dancer, so it may help to keep that in mind for remembering the kana.

HE へ: this sounds like the "he" in the name Helen. In order to remember this kana, think about Mr. Saint Helens.

HO ほ: this is pronounced just like ho. This visualization for remembering the kana may be a bit disturbing, but I'll bet you won't forget it. On the left side you have a chimney, and then on the right is a mutated-looking Santa. His head had been chopped off; he has a snake tail and four arms. Out of the space where his head should be, he is shouting, "ho, ho, ho."

- **まみむめも** ma-mi-mu-me-mo and **やゆよ** ya-yu-yo

MA **ま**: this makes the "ma" sound as in "magic" or "mama." In fact, you may be able to use the visualization of a really mind ma looking like the kana.

MI **み**: this is pronounced like "me." This looks like the number 21, so think about a person who just turned 21 going to Vegas and being asked who hit the jackpot and shouting, "Me, me, me."

MU **む**: this sounds just like a cow's moo. You can also look at the kana and see a cow.

ME **め** : this sounds like the "me" in "meh." If you look at the kana, it looks like an eye, and guess what the Japanese word for eye is, **め**.

MO **も**: this sounds like the "mo" in "more." This looks like a hook with several worms on it. So, if you really want to catch a fish, you add "more" worms.

YA や : this sounds like the "ya" in "yak," and when you look at the kana, it looks like a yak.

YU ゆ: this sounds like the "u" in "unique." The kana looks like a fish, so you can remember this as a unique fish.

YO よ: this sounds just like "yo." The kana looks like somebody hitchhiking, so think about a hitchhiker shouting, "yo, yo."

- らりるれろ ra-ri-ru-re-ro and わをんwa-wo-n

RA ら: this sounds like the "ra" in "rapper." To remember this, you can see the rapper at a DJ table in the kana.

RI り: this sounds like the "ree" in "reeds." You can look at the kana and picture it as reeds swaying in the wind.

RU る: this sounds just like "ru," such as rules. View this kana as a road, and it would be like driving a crazy route.

RE れ: this sounds like the "re" in "retching." You can look at the kana and see somebody kneeling and retching.

RO ろ: this sounds just like it looks, "ro." This looks like る, except for the fact it doesn't have a loop. Think about this one as an easy stream where you are rowing.

WA わ: this sounds like the "wa" in "wasp." You can look at this kana and see the angry little bee in it.

WO を: while it does sound like "whoa," it tends to be spoken more like "oh."

N ん: this is the only kana that represents a single kana, although to type it, you have to type in "nn" to get the character. It looks like and sounds like a lowercase "n."

That's the last of the hiragana, but now, we have to add in the dakuten. Dakuten adds a symbol that changes its pronunciation. These symbols typically look similar to a quotation mark, though there will be times when it will be a small circle. Here are the kana:

GA が GI ぎ GU ぐ GE げ GO ご

Luckily, there are only five rows of this, and the only thing you really need to know is the sound changes since you have already learned the kana.

Each of the kana in the か column can have a dakuten. This causes all of the "k" sounds to turn into "g" sounds.

KA か to GA が
KI き to GI ぎ
KU く to GU ぐ
KE け to GE げ
KO こ to GO ご

The next column that gets its own dakuten is the さ column. Here, the s changes to a z, except for し which changes to j.

SA さ to ZA ざ
SHI し to JI じ

SU す to ZU ず

SE せ to ZE ぜ

SO そ to ZO ぞ

The t-column gets changed to the d, except for the exceptions in this group.

TA た to DA だ

CHI ち to DI ぢ

TSU つ to ZU づ

TE て to DE で

TO と to DO ど

The exceptions in this column, ぢand づ, do not show up very often.

The next column to change is the は column. There are two different types of dakuten that you can use. One of them is the quotation symbol that we have been using, and the other is a circle.

HA は to BA ば or PA ぱ

HI ひ to BI び or PI ぴ

HU ふ to BU ぶ or PU ぷ

HE へ to BE べ or PE ぺ

HO ほ to BO ぼ or PO ぽ

You have to make sure you pay attention to this column because the H can become a B or a P.

Alright, we are almost done with this section. We have one more thing to go over. There isn't really anything new you have to learn here, but you will have to combine some of the kanas together to create new sounds. This will use things from the い row. This deals with small kana, such as:

や ゃ

ゆ ゅ

よ ょ

These get combined with other kana from the い row. The "I" is typically dropped, and it will turn into a single-syllable sound. Here they are:

- KYA きゃ
- KYU きゅ
- KYO きょ
- GYA ぎゃ
- GYU ぎゅ

- GYO ぎょ
- SHA しゃ
- SHU しゅ
- SHO しょ
- JYA じゃ
- JYU じゅ
- JYO じょ
- CHA ちゃ
- CHU ちゅ
- CHO ちょ
- NYAにゃ
- NYU にゅ
- NYO にょ
- HYA ひゃ
- HYU ひゅ
- HYO ひょ
- BYA びゃ
- BYU びゅ
- BYO びょ
- PYA ぴゃ
- PYU ぴゅ
- PYO ぴょ

- MYA みゃ
- MYU みゅ
- MYO みょ
- RYA りゃ
- RYU りゅ
- RYO りょ

That's it for the hiragana. As you practice, and the more you learn, you will figure out little differences and tricks. Let's move onto the next part of the kana you need to understand.

KATAKANA

Now, you have learned the hiragana, but guess what? You get to do the same thing all over again with the katakana.

Katakana Chart

•	w	r	y	m	h	n	t	s	k	
ン	ワ	ラ	ヤ	マ	ハ	ナ	タ	サ	カ	ア
n/m	wa	ra	ya	ma	ha	na	ta	sa	ka	a
		リ		ミ	ヒ	ニ	チ	シ	キ	イ
		ri		mi	hi	ni	chi	shi	ki	i
		ル	ユ	ム	フ	ヌ	ツ	ス	ク	ウ
		ru	yu	mu	fu	nu	tsu	su	ku	u
		レ		メ	ヘ	ネ	テ	セ	ケ	エ
		re		me	he	ne	te	se	ke	e
	ヲ	ロ	ヨ	モ	ホ	ノ	ト	ソ	コ	オ
	o	ro	yo	mo	ho	no	to	so	ko	o

27

While the same sounds of the hiragana are represented in the katakana (カタカナ), it is mostly used to write out foreign words. When it comes to foreign names, they are written with katakana, as well as foods. The quirky and fun onomatopoetic nature of Japan is seen in hiragana and katakana. The katakana characters look boxier than hiragana characters, and they are simpler than kanji. There is a hiragana counterpart to all katakana characters, which means they sound the same.

Since katakana is used for foreign words, the words won't always sound like the original. You will get used to it, though, and you will be able to understand how to say foreign words in Japanese sounds. Katakana is also used for things like:

- "robot-speech"
- Onomatopoeia
- When a person wants to emphasize something
- Company names
- Foods
- Animal
- Scientific
- For other stylistic reasons

Here are some names in katakana:

スティー・ブンキング – Stephen King

シェール – Cher

ジョン・ハンコック – John Hancock

When you look at the names, you'll notice a small dot between the names. It acts as a space between the first and last names so that Japanese readers can figure out where the names start and end.

Here are some other examples of foreign words written in katakana, while the remaining is in hiragana. The bolded symbols are katakana.

私わ**アメリカンフットボウル**がすき (watashi wa amerikanfuttoboru ga sukidesu) – "I like **American football**."

マクドナルドで食べる (makudonarudo de taberu) – "Eat at **McDonald's**."

ビールお飲みましょう(Biru o nomimashou) - "Let's drink **beer**."

Since the bolded words above aren't native to Japanese, they will be written in katakana. Words that represent sound, like sound effects used in anime or animal noises, will be also be written out in katakana as well.

Since you already know the sounds, we won't go over that. We'll just learn the kana for the katakana.

- A ア
- I イ
- U ウ
- E エ
- オ
- KA カ
- KI キ
- KU ク
- KE ケ
- KO コ
- SA サ
- SHI シ
- SU ス
- SE セ

- SO ソ
- TA タ
- CHI チ
- TSU ツ
- TE テ
- TO ト
- NA ナ
- NI ニ
- NU ヌ
- NE ネ
- NO ノ
- HA ハ
- HI ヒ
- FU フ
- HE ヘ
- HO ホ
- MA マ
- MI ミ
- MU ム
- ME メ
- MO モ
- YA ヤ

- YU ユ
- YO ヨ
- RA ラ
- RI リ
- RU ル
- RE レ
- RO ロ
- WA ワ
- WO ヲ
- N ン

Katakana has its own dakuten as well, but they work exactly like the dakuten of the hiragana. The sounds translate exactly the same; the only difference is you use the katakana symbol and add the quotation mark to the side of it.

Let's move onto the other small combinations within the katakana. These are very similar to the hiragana, but there are some combinations that get weird.

- KYA キャ
- KYU キュ
- KYO キョ

- GYA ギャ
- GYU ギュ
- GYO ギョ
- SHA シャ
- SHU シュ
- SHO ショ
- JYA ジャ
- JYU ジュ
- JYO ジョ
- CHA チャ
- CHU チュ
- CHO チョ
- NYA ニャ
- NYU ニュ
- NYO ニョ
- HYA ヒャ
- HYU ヒュ
- HYO ヒョ
- BYA ビャ
- BYU ビュ
- BYO ビョ
- PYA ピャ

- PYU ピュ
- PYO ピョ
- MYA ミャ
- MY ミュ
- MYO ミョ
- RYA リャ
- RYU リュ
- RYO リョ

This is where things start to get weird in the combinations for the katakana. There are several sounds used in non-Japanese languages that katakana has to be able to cover. "V" is a very common sound that the Japanese have to account for even though they don't use this sound. These are the closest you will find. You will notice that vowel sounds, which are in small letters, are added to produce these sounds.

- VA (BWA) ビァ
- VI (BWI) ビィ
- VU (BU) ブ
- VE (BWE) ビェ
- VO (BWO) ビォ

The "w" sound has to also be taken care of. As you can see, this is a sound that's not really covered, and it is only used as a particle. WI, WE, and WO can be written as follows.

- UI （WI） ウィ
- UE (WE) ウェ
- UO (WO) ウォ

The next sound that we have to cover is the "f" sound. The only syllable in Japanese that uses the "f" sound is fu. You can create the other "f" sounds, again, by combining with the vowel sounds, written in small letters.

- FA ファ
- FI フィ
- FE フェ
- FO フォ

Besides what we have covered, there are some other obscure sounds that have to be covered as well. The rest of them are:

- SHE シェ

- JE ジェ
- CHE チェ
- TSA ツァ
- TSI ツィ
- TSE ツェ
- TSO ツォ

These will be seen pretty often, but right now, just try to learn how to read them. You will get the hang of them the more you say and use them.

One last thing, unlike hiragana, which just adds more vowels to make up for long vowels, katakana uses a vowel extender. This is a simple dash. When you see the dash used, it simply means you need to extend the vowel. KO コ becomes KOU コー. Now, you know the Japanese alphabet. Once you have a good understanding of hiragana and katakana, you will find everything else to be much easier.

MEMORIZING KATAKANA AND HIRAGANA

Chances are, you would probably rather be on Facebook, watching TV, or doing just about anything other than learning katakana and hiragana. Luckily, there are just a few simple steps in learning these different scripts.

The next thing you should probably think about doing is making yourself a copy of a katakana and hiragana chart so that you have it as a reference. Once you have that, you should make sure that your computer is ready for you to write and read in Japanese. Most computers already have this ability; you just need to tell it to let you. There are many easy-to-follow tutorials online.

One of the best ways to help yourself learn katakana and hiragana is to type in Japanese whenever you have the chance. This could be when you are taking notes, tweeting something, or writing to somebody.

Once you have set your computer up to type in Japanese to begin typing, you will need to select Japanese as your input method. Type like you normally would on your keyboard. When you do this, and you type the letter a, you are going to get the character あ. That symbol represents the sound "a." If you were to type in "k-o," you are going to get the character こ.

Once you are completely satisfied with what you have written out, you can press the enter button. If you want to change what you have written from hiragana to katakana, all you need to do is hit the spacebar. You will then get a drop-down menu with different possibilities of kanji or katakana to pick from. Also, you do not ever need to press the spacebar between words. In Japanese, it is all written out together. This will help you to learn and recognize the different characters.

READING AND WRITING JAPANESE

Once you have gotten used to typing in Japanese, you should be able to recognize more characters, and then you can start to use pen and paper to write things out in Japanese. This is what will help to engrave each character into your mind. Create your own flashcards and keep a small journal so that you can regularly practice your Japanese.

You can even start to write out your daily activities in Japanese so that you will have to actively recall the characters. Chances are when you first start writing Japanese longhand, you will hate the way the characters look. But, the more you write them out, the better they will look.

Now, the biggest challenge is probably reading Japanese. You will read slowly when you first start, and it will probably be frustrating, but stick with it. The words will be hard to pronounce at first, but don't give up. You may also want to use a Furigana plugin on your web browser. This will place hiragana over unfamiliar kanji when you hover over the word. This will help you out when you haven't quite learned all of the kanji.

Chapter 3

THE BASICS OF GRAMMAR

The Japanese sentence structure is very different from English. I'm going to give you what I consider to be a cheat sheet. This first section will provide you with a broad explanation of the most common Japanese sentence patterns and how to change them from positive to negative statements. This will be something you can easily look back on if you get confused. After the "cheat sheet," we will go into the sentence structure and grammar in more depth. I feel that broadly going over the information before getting into the nitty-gritty is easier for most because you go into it already knowing the basics.

BASIC SENTENCE STRUCTURES

Affirmative and Declarative Sentences

In the broadest of terms, Japanese sentences fall into one of the three patterns.

1. Noun Phrase: "I am a Japanese person." Watashi wa Nihon-jin desu. 私和日本人です

2. Adjective Phrase: "Mary-san is busy." Mearisan wa isogashii desu.
   メアリーさんわ忙しいです

3. Verb Phrase: "Tanaka-san eats ramen." Tanaka-san wa ramen o tabemasu.
   田中さんわら面お食べます

"Desu" works similarly to the English phrase "to be," and will come at the end of adjective and noun phrases. Verb phrases tend to en with –masu.

The particle "wa" denotes the subjects and topics. "Ga" is another particle that can indicate the subject.

Negative Sentences

You can make negative sentences by modifying the

end of a predicate, which is normally the last section of a sentence. The grammatical structure is why you have to listen to the end of the sentence in Japanese to figure out if it is affirmative or negative.

1. Negative Noun Phrase: "I **am not** a Japanese person." Watashi wa Nihon-jin **jya-arimasen**. 私和日本人じゃありません

2. Negative Adjective Phrase: "Mary-San **is not** busy." Meari-San wa isogashi**ku nai desu**. メアリーさんは忙しくないです

3. Negative Verb Phrase: "Tanaka-San **does not** eat ramen." Tanaka-San wa ramen o ta-be**masen**. 田中さんはら面お食べません

Interrogative or Question Sentences

To make a sentence a question, you attach "ka" to the end of a declarative sentence.

1. "Is Mary-san busy?" Meari-san wa isogashii desu **ka**. メアリーさんわ忙しいです**か**

2. "Does Tanaka-San eat ramen?" Tanaka-san wa ramen o tabemasu **ka**. 田中さんわら面お食べます**か**

When you start to create longer sentences in Japanese, it normally requires you to insert different types of information between the subject and predicate. Particles help to simplify this.

PARTICLES

Particles in Japanese are a lot like the English prepositions, such as "at" and "in." As you will see below, while English will have prepositions, which come before the phrase they modify, clause, or noun, the Japanese will use postpositions, which will come after the phrase or clause.

1. "We had dinner **in** his room." Kare no heya **de** bangohon o tabemashita.
   彼の部屋で晩御飯お食べました
2. "I wake up **at** six o'clock every morning." Maisasa roku-ji-**ni** okimasu.
   舞佐々六時に起きます

While the particles don't actually carry any meaning, they do serve an important purpose in sentence formation. For example, in the English language, we do not use particles and simply rely on word order in the sentence. When you change the order of the words in an English sentence, it can cause the meaning of the sentence to change.

I gave my kid a cookie. I gave my cookie a kid.

However, the most important thing in a Japanese sentence isn't the order of the words. Instead, the important thing is the units of information made up of the particle and the phrase it modifies, noun, or clause.

Kodomo **ni** kukki **o** agemashita = Kodomo **o** kukki **ni** agemashita (I gave my child a cookie.)

子供にくっきお上げました=
子供おくっきえに上げました

Even if you change up the words of a sentence, as long as the particles stay the same, the meaning doesn't change all that much. Particles come in two different types. We are going to discuss the different particles and their purpose.

WA – は

Before I begin explaining this particle, this WA is not the わ that you get when typing in Japanese. This is actually the HA kana, は. There is a long drawn out explanation as to why the particle WA using the kana for HA, but the important thing right now is to remember that when WA stands alone as a particle, it should be written using the kana HA.

Let's go back to what we are talking about, with example sentences using the particle WA.

1. Subject: "I am a Thai person." Watashi wa Tai-jin desu. 私はタイ人です

2. "This costs 500 yen." Kore wa gohyaku-en desu. これは五百円です

3. Topic: "Yesterday, I went to an izakaya." Kino wa izakaya ni ikimashita.
   木野は居酒屋に行きました

4. "What did you do over the summer break?" Natsu-yasumi wa nani o shimashita ka.
   夏休み花に押しましたか

5. Comparisons: "I like sushi, but I don't like sashimi." Sushi wa suki desu ga, sashimi wa kirai desu. 寿司はすくですが刺身は嫌いです

O (WO) – を

1. Object: "I read newspapers." Shimbun o yomimasu. 新聞を読みます
2. "I drink coffee." Kohi o nomimasu. コーヒーを飲みます

NI – に

1. Object: "I'm going to see my friend." Tomodachi ni aimasu. 友達に会います
2. "I'm going to give my dad a necktie." Chichi ni nekutai o agemasu.
   父にネクタイを上げます
3. Destination: "I'm going to China." Chugoku ni ikimasu. 中国に行きます
4. "I'm coming to Japan." Nihon ni kimasu.
   日本に来ます
5. "I'm going back home." Uchi ni kaerimasu.
   うちに帰ります

When it comes to destinations, the particle "e" is often used to indicate a general direction and a destination and can be used interchangeably with "ni."

6. Time: "I get up at seven o'clock." Shichi-ji ni okimasu. 七時に起きます

7. "I go to be at eleven o'clock." Juichi-ji ni nemasu. 十一時に寝ます

8. "I'll come back at three o'clock." San-ji ni modorimasu. 三時に戻ります

9. Location: "There's a TV in my little brother's room." Ototo no heya ni terebi ga arimasu. 弟の部屋にテレビがあります

DE – で

1. Action place: "I eat dinner at restaurants." Resutoran de bangohan o tabemasu. レストランで盤語派を食べます

2. Means: "I'll go by bus." Basu de ikimasu. バスで行きます

3. Selection: Waiter: "Would you like bread or rice?" "Bread, please." Pan de onegaishimasu. (I'd like bread.) パンでお願いします

NO – の

You can use の to show possession of an object. The example sentences you will show that this is one of the easier sentence patterns to remember and learn.

1. Possession: "My car." Watashi no kuruma.
   私の車

2. "My friend's book." Tomodachi no hon.
   友達の本

You can also use の to show affiliation to an organization, like with the following sentences.

3. Affiliation: "An employee of _." _no shain.
   _の社員

4. A student of _." _no gakusei. _の学生

You can also use の to describe an attribute of the identity of something. Much like with the English language, we can say that a person is a "Japanese teacher," using の much in the same way.

5. Attribution: "Japanese teacher." Nihongo no sensei. 日本語の先生

6. "Strawberry sherbert." Ichigo no shabetto. いちごのしゃべっと

You can also use の to show apposition. This is when two people have a relationship.

7. Apposition: "My friend yoko." Tomodachi no yoko-san. 友達の横さ
8. "My husband, Tom." Otto no tomu. 夫のトム

The particle の has one more use, and that is as a pronoun. There is a similar pattern in English as well, such as "the _ one."

9. Pronoun: "The red one." Akai no. 赤いの
10. "The hot one." Atsui no. 暑いの

TO – と

The particle と can be used to show a partnership in action, or it can be used to form pairs. It can also be used like the conjunction "and." These are a few ways you can use this particle.

1. "I saw a movie with my friend." Tomodachi to eiga o mimashita. 友達と映画をっ見ました

2. "I married Eri-san." Eri-san to kekkon shimashita. エリさんと結婚しました

3. "I will speak with the CEO." Shacho to hanashimasu. 社著と話します

4. Parallel phrases: "Bread and eggs." Pan to tomago パンと卵

MO – も

This particle is used to show agreement and similarity. You can also use it to add emphasis to a certain statement.

1. Agreement or Sameness: "I'll have this, too, please." Kore mo onegaishimasu.
   これもお願いします

2. "I also like movies." Watashi mo eiga ga suki desu. 私も映画がすくです

3. Emphasis: "I drank five bottles of wine." Wain o go-hon mo nomimashita.
   ワインをご本も飲みました

KARA – から

This is used to show the origin of motion or duration.

1. "It takes 30 minutes to get from our house to the school." Uchi kara gakko made sanguppun kakarimasu.

うちから学校まで三十分かかります

MADE – まで

The particle まで is used just like KARA to signify the endpoint of motion or duration.

1. "I study from nine until eleven o'clock." Ku-ji kara juichi-ji made benkyo shimasu.

久慈から儒一時までべんきょします

GA – が

You can use this particle in several different ways. While it typically follows the subject, it can sometimes provide a function that is similar in nature to other particles. Since this makes GA confusing, try to keep in mind the following five patterns.

1. The Subject of an Interrogative Sentence with an Interrogative Word: "Who is coming?" Dare ga kimasu ka. 誰が来ますか

2. "When would be a good time?" Itsu ga ii desu ka. いつがいいですか

3. The Subject that Denotes Location or Possession: "We have a computer at our home." Uchi ni pasokon ga arimasu.

うちにパソコンがあります

4. "There is a cat in the restroom." Toire ni neko ga imasu. トイレに猫がいます

5. Embedded Clause Subject Modifying a Noun Phrase: "This is a piece of music that is composed by Beethoven." Kore wa Betoben ga tsukutta kyoku desu.

これはベートーヴェンが作った曲です

6. Objects: be bad at, dislike, be good at, and like. Heta, kirai, jouzu, suki.

下手、嫌い、上手、好き

   a. "I like soccer." Sakka ga suki desu.
   サッカが好きです

7. Can hear, can do, can see, and understand. Kikoeru, dekiru, mieru, wakaru.

聞こえる、できる、見える、わかる

   a. "It is possible to see Mount Fuji from here." Koko kara Fuji-san o miru koto ga dekimasu.

ここから富士山を見ることができます

8. Want to do, want/need. Shitai, hoshii.
   したい、ほしい

   a. "I want to study Japanese." Nihongo ga benkyou shitai desu.

      日本語が勉強したいです

   b. "I want a new TV." Atarashii terebi ga hoshii desu. 新しいテレビが欲しいです

9. The Aspect of the Subject: "My younger sister has long hair." Imoto wa kami ga nagai.
   妹うはかみが長い

ADVANCED GRAMMAR

You're probably thinking, "That' was a lot of grammar for it to be basic and simple." You're right; it was, but we are going to dive into picking apart what we talked about so that you understand the grammar aspects of Japanese better.

Expressing the State-of-Being

Declaring something is something with だ (DA).

Important vocabulary for this section:

1. Person – Hito, 人
2. Student – Gakusei, 学生
3. Healthy/Lively – Genki, 元気

A tricky part of Japanese is that they don't have a verb that matches up with the English, "to be." However, you are able to declare what something is by attaching だ to na-adjective or noun only. Here are some examples:

1. Is person: Hitoda 人だ
2. Is a student: Gakuseida 学生だ
3. Is well: Genkida 元気だ

This seems simple, right? Here's the fun part; you can imply a state-of-being without using だ. You have the ability to tell someone you are doing well or that a person is a student without using だ. You will see some examples below of what a typical conversation between friends might look like. Also, make sure you take note that the subject is not specified when there is an obvious context.

A casual greeting:

Friend 1: "(Are you) well?" Genki. 元気
Friend 2: "(I'm) well." Genki. 元気

The biggest difference is that declarative sentences come off as more forceful in order to make it declarative. This means that you will hear men use DA more often at the end of their sentences. DA is also important for different structures in grammar when you need to declare a state-of-being. There may be times where you can't attach it at all. This has a tendency to become a pain, but you don't have to face this problem just yet.

Conjugating Negative State-of-Being

Important vocabulary for this section:

1. Student: Gakusei 学生
2. Friend: Tomodachi 友達
3. Healthy/Lively: Genki 元気

You have to express past tense and negatives in Japanese through conjugation. An adjective or noun can be conjugated to its past tense or negative form by saying something is not (something) or was (something). This will sound confusing to start with, but none of these will make the sentence declarative as DA does. That will come later.

To make something negative, you have to add janai (じゃない) to a na-adjective or noun. Here are some examples:

1. Is not well. Genkijanai. 元気じゃない
2. Is not a friend. Tomodachijanai.
   友達じゃない
3. Is not a student. Gakuseijanai. 学生じゃない

Conjugating Past State-of-Being

Important vocabulary for this section:

1. Student: Gakusei. 学生
2. Friend: Tomodachi. 友達
3. Healthy/Lively: Genki. 元気

In order to say something in the past tense, you will add datta (だった) to the na-adjective or noun. When you want to say the negative past, you will need to conjugate the negative with the negative past tense by removing the い from じゃない and add a かった. For example:

1. Was not well. Genki janakatta.
   元気じゃなかった
2. Was not a friend. Tomodachi janakatta.
   友達じゃなかった
3. Was not a student. Gakusei janakatta.
   きれいじゃなかった

MORE ABOUT PARTICLES

You now understand how to provide a state-of-being within every tense. Next, we are going to look at particles, which give you the chance to assign roles to words. Now, we want to use what we have learned so far by associating one noun with another. This is where particles come in. Particles define the grammatical function of a certain word within a sentence. It is important to make sure you use the correct particles in sentences.

は Particle:

Important vocabulary for this section:

1. Student: Gakusei 学生
2. Yes: Un うん

は is what is known as a topic particle. This shows what you are talking about, basically, your sentence's topic. If somebody were to say, "Not student," that would be seen as a complete sentence in Japanese, but it doesn't fill us in on what is actually going on. When you use a topic particle, you will be able to express what you are talking about.

Bob, "Is Alice (you) a student?" Bobu: Arisu wa gakuseika. ボブ：アリスは学生課

Alice, "Yeah, (I) am." Arisu: Un, gakusei. アリス：うん、学生

In the first sentence, Bob is showing us that his question is about Alice. After the topic has been established, Alice doesn't need to repeat what the topic is in order to answer the question.

も Particle:

Important vocabulary for this section:

1. Student: Gakusei 学生
2. Yes: Un うん
3. No: Un ううん

This particle works a lot like the topic particle. MO is what is known as an inclusive topic particle. Basically, the topic particle gets an extra meaning. It can introduce the current and a new topic. The best way to understand this particle is to show you an example.

Bob, "Is Alice (you) a student?" Bobu: Arisu wa gakuseika. ボブ：アリスは学生課

Alice, "Yeah, and Tom is also a student." Arisu: Un, Tomu mo gakusei. アリス：うん、トムも学生

When you add in this particle, you have to make sure it is consistent with the answer. It wouldn't make any sense if you were to say, "I am a student, and Tom is also a student." In this case, you would use the は particle to break the answer.

が Particle

Important vocabulary for this section:

1. Who: dare 誰
2. Student: gakusei 学生
3. I/Myself/Me: watashi 私

We now have two particles to set the topic of a sentence, but what happens if we are unsure as to what the topic is? What we need now is an identifier because there will be times when you don't know who or what you are talking about. If you chose to use a topic particle, your sentence might come out as, "Is who the student?" This wouldn't make any sense because "who" isn't the topic.

This is where you will use が. This is what is called a subject particle, but the words subject in this context is very different from what a subject is in the English grammar. Maybe, a better way to refer to this particle would be to call it an identifier particle since it helps to tell that the speaker is trying to identify someone or something.

For example:

Bob: "Who is the student?" Bobu: Dare ga gakusei.
ボブ：誰が学生

Alice: "John is the one who is a student." Arisu: Jon ga gakusei. アリス：ジョンが学生

Bob is looking to find out who the student is. Alice tells him that a particular student is John. Alice also could have answered using the topic particle and said that she knows that John was a student.

ADJECTIVES

Now, we are moving on to adjectives. We can connect nouns in lots of different ways through the use of particles, but we now need to know how to describe the nouns using adjectives. Adjectives directly modify nouns that it follows. You can connect them in the same way as we did with the particles. There are two types of adjectives: i-adjectives and na-adjectives.

Na-Adjectives

These are the simplest adjectives to learn because they

act a lot like nouns. The conjugation rules that are used for nouns are also used for na-adjectives. The main difference between the two is that a na-adjective is able to modify a noun that comes after it by adding な between the adjective and noun. This is why they are called na-adjectives.

Here's an example:

1. "Quiet person." Shizukana hito. 静かな人
2. "Pretty person." Kireinahito. きれいな人

You are also able to use adjectives with the particles that we talked about earlier, just like you can with the nouns.

1. "Friend is a kind person." Tomodachi wa shinsetsu. 友達は親切
2. "My friend is kind." Tomodachi wa shinsetsu-na hitoda. 友達は親切な人だ

I-Adjectives

I-adjectives will always end in い, hence the name. However, you could be saying that there are some na-

63

adjectives that end in い as well. So how can we figure out the difference? There aren't all that many na-adjectives that also end in い that aren't typically written in kanji. Nearly all na-adjectives that have the ending of い will typically be written in kanji, which will help you to tell them apart from the i-adjectives. Unlike the other adjectives, i-adjectives don't need to have な added to modify a noun.

1. "Tasty food." Oishi tabemono.
   おいしい食べ物
2. "Hated food." Kirainatabemono.
   嫌いな食べ物

Remember the nouns with a negative state-of-being ended with い? Much like those nouns, you aren't allowed to attach the declarative だ to these i-adjectives. Now, let's go over how to conjugate i-adjectives.

- For negatives: get rid of the い and then add くない. For example, 高い becomes 高くない.

- For past-tense: take off the い and then add on かった. For example, 高い becomes 高かった.

You didn't think we could make it this far without a single exception. There is an i-adjective that means "good," and it does things a bit differently than the other i-adjectives. This is one of the main reasons that beginners struggle with learning Japanese because the most common words tend to have more exceptions. Originally, the word for "good" was yoi よい. Over time, though, it turned into ii いい. The problem is all of the conjugations of いい are still derived from よい.

This isn't the only word that acts like that this. Kakkoi かっこいい is another one. The reason for this is that it is an abbreviation of two words that have been merged. Since it has いい in it, you have to use the same conjugations that we'll go over.

Conjugations for いい:

- Not Past Tense Positive: いい
- Not Past Tense Negative: よくない (yokunai)

- Past Tense Positive: よかった (yokatta)
- Past Tense Negative: よくなかった (yokuna-katta)

Conjugation for かっこいい:

- Not Past Tense Positive: かっこいい
- Not Past Tense Negative: かっこよくない (kakkoyokunai)
- Past Tense Positive: かっこよかった (kakko-yokatta)
- Past Tense Negative: かっこよくなかった (kakkoyokunakatta)

Alright, that's it for the grammar, well, mostly. We still have to talk about verbs, but they get their own chapter.

Chapter 4

THE BASICS IN VERBS

We have gone over nouns and how to describe them in many different ways with other adjectives and nouns. You have a lot of power to express things now. However, we still haven't gone over how to express action. This is why we need verbs. In Japanese, you will place verbs at the end of a clause. Since we haven't talked about creating more than a single clause, all you need to remember is that any sentence with an action needs to end with a verb. We are going to go over the three main types of verbs, which also defines the conjugation rules. Before we jump into the verbs, there is something that you need to know.

To have a grammatically complete sentence, you only need a verb. To say it another way, unlike with English, the only thing a grammatically correct Japanese sentence needs is a verb. This is the reason that the most basic sentence in Japanese cannot be translated into English.

Here is an example of this:

Taberu 食べる: This means "Eat," but in English, we would likely say "They eat," "She eats," or "I eat."

Before we start conjugating verbs, we have to learn the two verb categories. Besides two exceptions, all verbs will fall into u-verbs and ru-verbs.

The ru-verbs will end in る. The u-verbs end in several u-vowel sounds, which include る. That means that if a verb doesn't en in る, it is going to be a u-verb. When the verb ends with a る and the vowel sound that comes before it is a, u, or o, it is going to be a u-verb. If it is preceded by i or e, it is going to be a ru-verb, most of the time. We will go over the exceptions later on.

So what should you do with this new information? Well, you can look at the RU and U part of the verbs that can be removed. You take those off, and then you have your verb stem, and that is what you need when it comes to conjugating the verbs. RU and U also let you know the options you have for conjugating the verbs.

CONJUGATING RU VERBS

The first verbs we are going to learn how to conjugate are RU verbs. We will start with taberu 食べる, which means "to eat." When you take off the RU, all you have left is tabe, the base form. From there, you can begin building something new. When you want your verb to be in the present tense, you will add masu at the end.

So we have removed the RU, and now, we are going to add masu to get tabemasu, 食べます. This means "I eat." It doesn't mean, "I am eating," because, in most languages, it would be present progressive tense. The good news, though, is that conjugation you just did works for present and future tense.

Here are a couple of other present/future tense RU verb conjugations.

To conjugate miru (見る), "to see," we will swap out the RU with masu to get mimasu (見ます).

To conjugate neru (寝る), "to sleep," you will get nemasu (寝ます).

Now, we have to put RU verbs into the past tense. You are going to drop the same RU and add mashita to the end. For the verbs we have already conjugated, we are going to have:

1. Tabemasu to tabemashita
2. Mimasu to mimashita
3. Nemasu to nemashita

All RU verbs will conjugate in this way. If you can remember this, you should be set for the conjugation of verbs.

Now, we have to look at the U-verbs, but they aren't all that different. Instead of just ripping off the U and replacing it with something else, you will have to look at what type of U it is. As you had already learned when we covered the kana, Japanese letters have little families. If you have the word kiku, it would be a part of the ku family. The word yomu belongs to the mu family. The main thing you need to remember is that U at the end of the word isn't always by itself. Then there are words like utau, where it is.

So, you will be taking the U off the end of the word, but depending on the family it is a part of, you will add something different to the end. You have to look back at the family to figure out which version you need to replace the U with.

We'll look at utau (歌う) first. Once the U is taken off, you are left with the stem uta. Don't throw the U away completely. Look back at the family. For this one, it would be a-i-u-e-o and then choose the i group. Then you will conjugate just what like you did with the RU verbs.

The present tense of utau is utaimasu (歌います), and the past tense would be utaimashita (歌いました).

So why do we need to pick the i group? We'll look at some other verbs to figure out why.

Kiku (聞く) "to listen," becomes kikimasu (聞きます) in present tense and kikimashita (聞きました) in the past tense.

Yomu (読む) "to read," becomes yomimasu (読みます) in present tense and yomimashita (読みました) in the past tense.

It was important to know the i member of their family in all of these so that you can have utai, and the ki in kiki, as well as the mi in the yomi. To look at this in simpler terms, you get rid of the U and place imasu or imashita to the end.

Before we slide into those exceptions that I know you have been looking forward to, let's go over some other verb conjugations that you would want to know.

- "I can't" emasen or raremasen. For example, miraremasen (見られません) "I can't see." Or, yomemasen (読めません) "I can't read."
- "I can" emasu or raremasu. For example, yomemasu (読めます) "I can read." Or, miraremasu (見られます) "I can see."

- "I don't want to." Itakuna or takunai. For example, utaitakunai (歌いたくない) "I don't want to sing." Or, tabetakunai (食べたくない) "I don't want to eat."
- "I want to." Itai (U-verbs) or tai (RU-verbs). For example, utaitai (歌いたい). Or, tabetai (食べたい) "I want to eat."

DISGUISED U-VERBS

Now, let's go over the exceptions. There are times when a verb that ends in RU can be a U verb in disguise. Hairu is one example. It means "to enter." You may be thinking that all you need to do is change it to *haimasu*. Not exactly. The present tense would actually ly be *hairimasu*. This is where a U-verb is working undercover.

Now, how are you going to know the difference? Unfortunately, the best way is simply to learn the exceptions. Some of the ones you may find are:

- To return: kaeru 帰る
- To know: shiru 知る

- To chat: shaberu しゃべる
- To need: iru いる

VERB IRREGULARITIES

There is one last exception. There are two irregular verbs. It is best to memorize them separately when you are starting out.

The first one is suru, meaning "to do." If you followed the rules for RU, you would get sumasu. While that does make sense, it isn't right. But, the U-verb rules are going to give you the right answer either way.

Suru conjugates to this:

- Shitakunai: したくない
- Saremasu: されます
- Shimashita: しました
- Shimasen: しません
- Shimasu: します

The second verb that follows suru's example is kuru, meaning "to come." It conjugates out to:

- Kitakunai: 来たくない

74

- Koraremasu: 来られます
- Kimashita: 来ました
- Kimasen: 来ません
- Kimasu: 来ます

That's it for the grammar, but you will learn more as we continue on. There are more verbs, nouns, and adjectives out there, but those will and can be learned through example texts and practice.

Chapter 5

LEARNING YOUR NUMBERS

We've made it through the boring parts of learning a new language; now, let's get into learning something just a bit more fun. We are going to learn the numbers. You need to know the numbers, right? The Japanese number system can seem very complex, especially for the beginner.

Basic counting Japanese is fairly easy, but there are many different ways to count, even just up to ten. When it comes to counting objects, it can get very confusing because of what is known as "counters." But we are going to go through all of it, and I will give you the best tricks and tips when it comes to counting in Japanese and working through the tricky parts.

ONE THROUGH TEN

There are two sets of numbers in the Japanese number system. There is the native Japanese number set and the Sino-Japanese number set. Sino-Japanese numbers are the most commonly used number, but it is not uncommon to come across the native numbers when looking at numbers one through ten.

- Sino-Japanese Numbers
- One – ichi いち : Kanji: 一
- Two – ni に: Kanji: 二
- Three – san さん: Kanji: 三
- Four – shi/yon し/よん: Kanji: 四
- Five – go ご: Kanji: 五
- Six – roku ろく : Kanji: 六
- Seven – shichi/nana しち/なな: Kanji: 七
- Eight – hachi はち: Kanji: 八
- Nine – ku/kyuu く/きゅう: Kanji: 九
- Ten – juu じゅう: Kanji: 十
- Zero – rei/zero/maru れい/ゼロ/まる: Kanji: 零
- Native Japanese Numbers
- One – hitotsu ひとつ: Kanji: 一つ

- Two – futatsu ふたつ: Kanji: 二つ
- Three – mittsu みっつ: Kanji: 三つ
- Four – yottsu よっつ: Kanji: 四つ
- Five – itsutsu いつつ: Kanji: 五つ
- Six – muttsu むっつ: Kanji: 六つ
- Seven – nanatsu ななつ: 七つ
- Eight – yattsu やっつ: Kanji: 八つ
- Nine – kokonotsu ここのつ: Kanji: 九つ
- Ten – tou とう: Kanji: 十

The good news is, you will only see the Native Number System used for the number one through ten, so it should make things easier. And the other cool thing about this number system is that it doesn't have any counters. We will go over counters in a moment, but this number set is considered to be the universal counter. These numbers can be used to count everything except for people, money, and time. If you find yourself stuck figuring out a number, you can use these.

The best way to remember these numbers is that every single one of them ends in tsu つ, except for the number ten, which is tou とう. This little trick also helps you to remember the kanji for this set of numbers. You will also be able to tell which counting system a person is using by whether or not the kanji has つ at the end, of course, except for ten.

Let's look over the Sino-Japanese number system. This is the group of numbers that will get the most use, and they will be the ones you combine with counters in order to count objects. Once you have memorized the numbers through ten, counting up to 100 is extremely easy. As you have probably already noticed, there are three numbers that have two different readings: four, seven, and nine. In Japanese, four and nine are both considered unlucky because し and く are the same sounds used for the words death, 死, and agony, 苦. Japanese people will often try to stay away from those readings whenever they can. Seven is considered a lucky number, but one of its readings is しち, which has shi in it, so they will most often use the other reading: なな.

When it comes to the number zero, the actual Japanese word is 例 (rei), but it is actually more common to simply say it like we do in English. Zero (ゼロ) is more often used, or they will use maru, which also means a circle and is very similar to the English expression of "oh" instead of zero.

COUNTING TO 100

Once you have learned the first ten numbers, getting yourself up to 100 is very easy. The good news is it also only uses one system. In Japanese, once you have passed the number ten, you start to count like you are adding. This is what it looks like:

11: juuichi 十一: 10 + 1
12: juuni 十二: 10 + 2

And it goes like that all the way up to 19. When you get to the number 20, you still follow the same concept, but you begin counting in tens.

20: nijuu 二十: two tens
21: nijuuichi 二十一: two tens plus one

And that continues on until you reach number 99.

Once you hit 100, that number gets its own new word: hyaku 百.

0	零	ぜろ、れい	Zero, rei
1	一	いち	Ichi
2	二	に	Ni
3	三	さん	San
4	四	よん、し	Yon, shi
5	五	ご	Go
6	六	ろく	Roku
7	七	しち、なな	Shichi, nana
8	八	はち	Hachi
9	九	きゅう、く	Kyû, ku
10	十	じゅう	Jû
11	十一	じゅういち	Jû-ichi
12	十二	じゅうに	Jû-ni
13	十三	じゅうさん	Jû-san

14	十四	じゅうよん、じゅうし	Jû-yon, jû-shi
15	十五	じゅうご	Jû-go
16	十六	じゅうろく	Jû-roku
17	十七	じゅうしち、じゅうなな	Jû-shichi, jû-nana
18	十八	じゅうはち	Jû-hachi
19	十九	じゅうきゅう	Jû-kyû
20	二十	にじゅう	Ni-jû
21	二十一	にじゅういち	Ni-jû-ichi
22	二十二	にじゅうに	Ni-jû-ni
23	二十三	にじゅうさん	Ni-jû-san
24	二十	にじゅうよん、にじゅ	Ni-jû-yon,

	四	うし	ni-jû-shi
25	二十五	にじゅうご	Ni-jû-go
26	二十六	にじゅうろく	Ni-jû-roku
27	二十七	にじゅうしち、にじゅうなな	Ni-jû-shichi, ni-jû-nana
28	二十八	にじゅうはち	Ni-jû-hachi
29	二十九	にじゅうきゅう	Ni-jû-kyû
30	三十	さんじゅう	San-jû
31	三十一	さんじゅういち	San-jû-ichi
32	三十二	さんじゅうに	San-jû-ni

33	三十三	さんじゅうさん	San-jû-san
34	三十四	さんじゅうよん、さんじゅうし	San-jû-yon, san-jû-shi
35	三十五	さんじゅうご	San-jû-go
36	三十六	さんじゅうろく	San-jû-roku
37	三十七	さんじゅうしち、さんじゅうなな	San-jû-shichi, san-jû-nana
38	三十八	さんじゅうはち	San-jû-hachi
39	三十九	さんじゅうきゅう	San-jû-kyû
40	四十	よんじゅう	Yon-jû
41	四十	よんじゅういち	Yon-jû-ichi

一

42	四十二	よんじゅうに	Yon-jû-ni
43	四十三	よんじゅうさん	Yon-jû-san
44	四十四	よんじゅうよん、よんじゅうし	Yon-jû-yon, yon-jû-shi
45	四十五	よんじゅうご	Yon-jû-go
46	四十六	よんじゅうろく	Yon-jû-roku
47	四十七	よんじゅうしち、よんじゅうなな	Yon-jû-shichi, yon-jû-nana
48	四十八	よんじゅうはち	Yon-jû-hachi
49	四十	よんじゅうきゅう	Yon-jû-kyû

九

50	五十	ごじゅう	Go-jû
51	五十一	ごじゅういち	Go-jû-ichi
52	五十二	ごじゅうに	Go-jû-ni
53	五十三	ごじゅうさん	Go-jû-san
54	五十四	ごじゅうよん、ごじゅうし	Go-jû-yon, go-jû-shi
55	五十五	ごじゅうご	Go-jû-go
56	五十六	ごじゅうろく	Go-jû-roku
57	五十七	ごじゅうしち、ごじゅうなな	Go-jû-shichi, go-jû-nana

58	五十八	ごじゅうはち	Go-jû-hachi
59	五十九	ごじゅうきゅう	Go-jû-kyû
60	六十	ろくじゅう	Roku-jû
61	六十一	ろくじゅういち	Roku-jû-ichi
62	六十二	ろくじゅうに	Roku-jû-ni
63	六十三	ろくじゅうさん	Roku-jû-san
64	六十四	ろくじゅうよん、ろくじゅうし	Roku-jû-yon, roku-jû-shi
65	六十五	ろくじゅうご	Roku-jû-go
66	六十	ろくじゅうろく	Roku-jû-

	六		roku
67	六十七	ろくじゅうしち、ろくじゅうなな	Roku-jû-shichi, roku-jû-nana
68	六十八	ろくじゅうはち	Roku-jû-hachi
69	六十九	ろくじゅうきゅう	Roku-jû-kyû
70	七十	ななじゅう	Nana-jû
71	七十一	ななじゅういち	Nana-jû-ichi
72	七十二	ななじゅうに	Nana-jû-ni
73	七十三	ななじゅうさん	Nana-jû-san
74	七十四	ななじゅうよん、ななじゅうし	Nana-jû-yon, nana-

			jû-shi
75	七十五	ななじゅうご	Nana-jû-go
76	七十六	ななじゅうろく	Nana-jû-roku
77	七十七	ななじゅうしち、ななじゅうなな	Nana-jû-shichi, nana-jû-nana
78	七十八	ななじゅうはち	Nana-jû-hachi
79	七十九	ななじゅうきゅう	Nana-jû-kyû
80	八十	はちじゅう	Hachi-jû
81	八十一	はちじゅういち	Hachi-jû-ichi
82	八十二	はちじゅうに	Hachi-jû-ni

二

83	八十三	はちじゅうさん	Hachi-jû-san
84	八十四	はちじゅうよん、はちじゅうし	Hachi-jû-yon, hachi-jû-shi
85	八十五	はちじゅうご	Hachi-jû-go
86	八十六	はちじゅうろく	Hachi-jû-roku
87	八十七	はちじゅうしち、はちじゅうなな	Hachi-jû-shichi, ha-chi-jû-nana
88	八十八	はちじゅうはち	Hachi-jû-hachi
89	八十九	はちじゅうきゅう	Hachi-jû-kyû

90	九十	きゅうじゅう	Kyû-jû
91	九十一	きゅうじゅういち	Kyû-jû-ichi
92	九十二	きゅうじゅうに	Kyû-jû-ni
93	九十三	きゅうじゅうさん	Kyû-jû-san
94	九十四	きゅうじゅうよん、きゅうじゅうし	Kyû-jû-yon, kyû-jû-shi
95	九十五	きゅうじゅうご	Kyû-jû-go
96	九十六	きゅうじゅうろく	Kyû-jû-roku
97	九十七	きゅうじゅうしち、きゅうじゅうなな	Kyû-jû-shichi, kyû-jû-nana
98	九十	きゅうじゅうはち	Kyû-jû-

	八		hachi
99	九十九	きゅうじゅうきゅう	Kyû-jû-kyû
100	百	ひゃく	Hyaku

The number 20 is hatachi (はたち). When a person turns 20, the Japanese considers a person to be an adult. The other irregularity to these numbers is hatsuka (はすか), which is the 20th day during the month.

ONE TO A TRILLION

When it comes to reading numbers, knowing the kanji will make it easier. The hiragana of numbers can end up getting pretty long, as you can see from above, and I'm sure you don't want to remember all of those kana. The kanji keeps things short and sweet. With the way the numbers work, you don't have to memorize a bunch of them either.

1	一	いち (ichi)
2	二	に (ni)
3	三	さん (san)
4	四	よん (yon)
5	五	ご (go)
6	六	ろく (roku)
7	七	なな (nana)
8	八	はち (hachi)
9	九	きゅう (kyuu)
10	十	じゅう (juu)
100	百	ひゃく (hyaku)
1,000	千	せん (sen)
10,000	万	まん (man)
100,000	十万	じゅうまん (juuman)

1,000,000	百万	ひゃくまん (hyakuman)
10,000,000	千万	せんまん (senman)
100,000,000	一億	いちおく (ichioku)
1,000,000,000	十億	じゅうおく (juuoku)
1,000,000,000,000	一兆	いっちょう (icchou)

As you can tell by looking at the kanji, the numbers continue to stack up all the way through the number one trillion and beyond. The main difference within all of these is that the larger numbers will be divided by units of four instead of three. Once you are past the number 10,000, it can be a little bit confusing when it comes to thinking of a million as "one hundred ten-thousands."

Here's a little bit of information. Nowadays, Japanese people will typically use the Romanized numbers that we all know when it comes to writing down numbers instead of the kanji. While they are mainly written the same as we write them in English, it is still important that you learn their kanji because they do sometimes pop up, especially if they are paired with other kanji characters.

MOST COMMON COUNTERS

I've mentioned them a couple of times, but what are counters? Counters are what specify the type of object that you are counting. Japanese has several forms of counters for every little thing—things that range from machinery to animals to long objects. This is probably one of the most confusing parts of learning Japanese. But, there are some tips and tricks to help you to learn them.

Like I mentioned earlier, if you aren't sure about the counter for a certain item, you have the option to use the native number system up to ten to count objects. This will help you to save some time and trouble when it comes to memorizing the numbers.

Another thing to remember is that some of the numbers will conjugate differently with different counters. The main ones to keep a lookout for are one, three, six, and eight. The number one will change half the time, and three, six, and eight will change most of the time. Three will change the first letter of counters that come from the "h" column in the kana to a "p" or "b" such as sanpun (三分), which means three minutes. Six will change the "h" kana to a "pp," such as roppiki (六匹), which means six animals. Eight will change the "h" counters just like the six, typically. This isn't really a rule, but they are common enough to help you when you are starting out.

There are times when the less common forms of four, seven, and nine will be used with specific counters, such as shichiji (七時), which means 7 o'clock.

Now, let's look at the most common counters that you need to know.

- People

  When it comes to counting people, you will use the counter nin 人 when you are counting three or more people. When you are counting one person, you would say hitori ひとり. For two people, you would say futari ふたり. All numbers after that are going to be the いち、

に、 さん number system, which will be followed by 人.

- Long objects

    When you are counting thin, long objects, such as bottles, pens, or chopsticks, you will use the counter hon 本. While in Japanese, hon means "book," it is not the counter you would use for books. When it comes to bound objects, like books, you will use satsu. Hon is also used when counting train tracks, rivers, and roads. Basically, anything that would be considered thin and long. You can also use this for long-distance phone calls, as well as travel routes. One example would be yon hon no pen 四本のペン, which means "four pens."

- Small objects

    To count small objects, you would use the counter ko 個. This is also used for objects that are round, such as apples.

- Animals

  When you are counting small animals, such as cats and dogs, you will use hiki匹. When it comes to larger animals, such as elephants or horses, you will use tou 頭. You could say sanbiki no inu 三匹の犬 to tell somebody you have "three dogs. Notice the h changed to b in hiki. You could say santou no uma 三頭の馬 to say you have "three horses."

- Mechanical objects

  Yes, video game consoles, dryers, washers, and cars have their own special counters in Japanese, as well as computers. Bicycles are also a part of this category, as well. For this category, you will use dai 台.

- Units of time

  You have to use counters to express time, as well. Seconds is expressed using byou 秒 , minutes is expressed with pun or fun 分, hours is expressed with ji 時, and length of time is express with jikan 時間.

For years, you would use nen 年, and for months, you would use getsu 月.

- Other counters

You may also see counters like mai 枚, kai 回, and gai/kai 階. Mai is most often used to count flat objects, such as paper. You would use kai to show the number of times you did something, like how many times you went to work out during the week. And gai is used to count how many floors a building has.

GRAMMAR ON NUMBERS

I told you grammar would come back. In Japanese, you can place the number after or before what you are counting. But, most of the time they will come after the item and particle, like hagaki wo gomai kaimasu はがきを五枚買います, which means "I will buy five postcards." はがき is the item counted, を is the particle, 五枚 is the number and counter, and買います is the verb.

If you were to place the number before the item being counted, you would have to use the particle of no. You would reverse the sentence to gomai no jagaki wo kaimasu 五枚のじゃがきを買います, which means the same thing, but it will place more emphasis on the quantity. You normal say it this way if you are answering a question.

One final note on counters: it is important that you don't get discouraged. They will seem hard, but in English, we use these types of counters as well. Think about it. For garlic, lettuce, or cabbage, we refer to them as heads. When it comes to fine or thin objects, we say strands, and pants and underwear come in pairs. There are some counters that are completely unique to a noun, like a skein of yarn. If you really stop to think about it, the Japanese counter system is more logical than English because they have a counter for every noun instead of select ones.

ORDINAL NUMBERS

Ordinal numbers are used to show sequence or order, such as first, second, and third. To do this in Japanese, you add dai 第. If you are saying "first," it would be dai ichi 第一 and so on.

When it comes to other numbers with counters that you want to place into a sequence, you will add me 目. If you were to say something like "for the first time," it would be ikkai me 一回目.

DAYS OF THE MONTH

After you have learned the counters, this is the next hardest part of the Japanese. The days of the month tend to be very inconsistent, especially when it comes to the first ten, as well as the 14th, 20th, and 24th. The first ten works a lot like the native counting system, but it isn't quite the same. So the best thing is to simply try to memorize them.

- Tsuitachi ついたち – 1st
- Futsuka ふつか – 2nd
- Mikka みっか – 3rd

102

- Yokka よっか – 4th
- Itsuka いつか – 5th
- Muika むいか – 6th
- Nanoka なのか – 7th
- Youka ようか – 8th
- Kokonoka ここのか – 9th
- Tooka とおか – 10th
- Juuyokka じゅうよっか – 14th
- Hatsuka はつか – 20th
- Nijuuyokka にじゅうよっか – 24th

All of the other numbers will follow the same stacking system.

Now, the last little bit we're going to go over in this chapter doesn't actually have to do with numbers, but if you are learning how the days of the week go, you might as well learn the names of the days of the week, as well as the months.

Months

- January: ichi gatsu いちがつ (一月)
- February: ni gatsu にがつ (二月)

103

- March: san gatsu さんがつ (三月)
- April: Shi gatsu しがつ (四月)
- May: Go gatsu ごがつ (五月)
- June: Roku gatsu ろくがつ (六月)
- July: Shichi gatsu しちがつ (七月)
- August: Hachi gatsu はちがつ (八月)
- September: Ku gatsu くがつ (九月)
- October: Ju gatsu じゅうがつ (十月)
- November: Juichi gatsu じゅういちがつ (十一月)
- December: Juni gatsu じゅうにがつ (十二月)

Days of the Week

- Monday: getsu yobi げつようび （月曜日）
- Tuesday: ka yobi かようび (火曜日)
- Wednesday: sui yobi すいようび (水曜日)
- Thursday: moku yobi もくようび (木曜日)
- Friday: kin yobi きんようび (金曜日)
- Saturday: do yobi どようび (土曜日)
- Sunday: niche yobi にちようび (日曜日)

Chapter 6

STARTING CONVERSATIONS

What do you have to do before you can ever start talking to somebody? Start the conversation. It doesn't matter if you are still working on grasping the kana, or you have gotten that under your belt and ready to start holding conversations. The thoughts of actually having a conversation can drive you crazy.

I get it. There are a lot of things going on in your mind, trying to remember the correct conjugation and so on, so thinking about initiating a conversation is at the bottom of the list. You're probably thinking, "Are they even going to understand me? What if I say something wrong? What if I don't know the word for what I am trying to tell them?"

These are all perfectly normal thoughts and reactions when it comes to mastering a language. Thankfully, you are going into your future conversations armed with a bunch of basic phrases to start conversations. These also work as great starting points when you are still learning the basics of Japanese. These will work as a backbone on which you can build your knowledge.

EIGHT MUST-KNOW GREETINGS

When you meet a person for the first time, you will normally start conversations with simple pleasantries like "it's nice to meet you" or "hello," right? Japanese has a lot of these basic phrases that you can use to begin a conversation. The next time you meet a new friend, why don't you try these on for size?

1. "Hello": *Konnichiwa* こんにちわ
2. "Good morning": *Ohayou gozaimasu* おはようございます
3. "Good evening": *Konbanwa* こんにちわ
4. "Hello": *Moshi moshi* もしもし – this is only used when talking to somebody on the phone or something like Skype

5. "How are you?": *Ogenki desu ka?* お元気ですか

6. "I'm good" or "I've been doing well, thanks": *Genki desu* 元気です

7. "Long time no see": *Ohisashiburi desu ne* お久しぶりですね

8. "_And you?": *_san mo?* _さんも – You would fill in the blank with the person's name. This is a good response when asked "how are you?" because you will be able to say, "I'm good. And you?"

9. "Nice to meet you": *Hajimemashite* 初めまして

FIVE PHRASES TO LEARN MORE ABOUT THE OTHER PERSON

Once you have greeted a person, it is likely you are going to get to know them. Let's keep that conversation rolling, shall we?

1. "What's your name?": *Namae wa nan desu ka?* 名前は何ですか

2. "My name is ___": *Watashi no namae wa* ___ *desu* 私の名前は__です

3. "Where are you from?": *Doko kara kimashita ka?* どこから来ましたか

4. "I'm from ___": *Watashi wa* ___ *kara kimashita* 私は__から来ました

5. "Is that so?" or "Really?" or "I see": *Sou desu ka?* そうですか – this is a good phrase to use after you have learned where a person is from, what they do, or any other fun facts about them.

6. "I am ___ years old": *Watashi wa* ___ *sai desu* 私は__さいです

SEVEN IMPORTANT POLITENESS PHRASES

You're doing great. You have introduced yourself and learned a little bit about the other person, and now, you can move on to something new. First, you can try out some traditional phrases that tend to be used early on during a conversation, plus others to have in your back pocket should you need them.

1. "Thank you": *Arigatou gozaimasu* ありがとうございます

2. "You're welcome": *Douitashimashite* どういたしまして

3. "I'm sorry" or "Excuse me": *Sumimasen* すみません— this can be used for apologizing for stumbling into a person, asking somebody for help, or asking people to move around, among others.

4. "I'm sorry": *Gomen nasai* ごめんなさい— this "I'm sorry" is used when you are truly sorry about something, and it isn't used for "excuse me." This is used for knocking over something and breaking it, not just interrupting their stroll to ask for directions.

5. "I'm in your debt": *Yoroshiku onegaishimasu* よろしくお願いします— this isn't typically used in the literal sense. It is simply a way of telling somebody, "thank you." For example, if you are beginning a new job, you could introduce yourself and tag this onto the end of the sentence. It can also be used if you have asked a favor of somebody.

6. "Let's dig in": *Itadakimasu* いただきます — this is something you can say before meals to politely say you are going to start enjoying the meal.

7. "That was delicious": *Gochisousama deshita* ごちそうさまでした — this is said after meals as a way to say thank you.

At this point, you should be able to have a conversation that goes something like this:

"Hi! Nice to meet you. I'm Aki. I'm 36 years old, and I've lived in Japan for six years."

- "Konnichiwa! Hajimemashite Aki desu. Watashi wa san juu roku sai de nihon ni wa roku nen sundeima."

- こんにちわ！はじめまして、秋です。私は三十六歳で日本医は六年住んでいま。

"Hi, Aki, nice to meet you. I'm Tomo. I've lived in Japan for a year and five years in Italy."

- "Konnichiwa Aki. Watashi wa Tomo desu. Nihon ni wa ichi nenkan sumi itariya ni wa go nenkan sundeimashita."
- こんにちわあき。わたしはともです。日本医は一年間住みイタリヤには五年間住んでいました。

"Italy sounds exciting."

- "Itariya wa tanoshisou desune."
- イタリヤは楽しそうですね

NINE CONVERSATION CLARIFIERS

Your conversation has been going on for a bit now, but what happens if all of your fears come true, and you start to get confused? First off, don't let yourself panic. Even when you are speaking in your native language, you have probably had to ask people to clarify a thing or two or repeat something. You aren't going to offend them. Just take things slowly.

1. "And in English, that's…?": Eigo te iu no wa 英語ていうのは

2. "I don't understand": Wakarimasen わかりません

3. "I don't know": Shirimasen 知りません

4. "I forgot": Wasuremashita 忘れました

5. "Please go a little slower": Motto yukkuri kudasai もっとゆっくりください

6. "Could you say that one more time?": Mou ichido kudasai もう一度下し

7. "I'm not very fluent in Japanese": Nihango de perapera de wa nai desu 二反語でペラペラではないです

8. "What does ___ mean?": ___ te iu no imi wa nan desu ka? ___ていうの意味は何ですか

9. "Can you help me?" Testsudatte kuremasen ka? 手伝ってくれませんか

SIX QUESTIONS YOUR MUST KNOW

Japanese is probably one of the easiest languages to ask questions, so ask whatever you want. The only thing you need to do to ask a question is to add ka to the end of the sentence. Remember that from an earlier chapter? Besides that, there are some questions words that can make conversations go smoother.

1. "Where is it?" Doko desu ka? どこですか
2. "When is it?" Itsu desu ka? いつですか
3. "Why?" Doushite? どうして
4. "Which one is it?" Dochira desu ka? どちらですか
5. "What is it?" Nan desu ka? 何ですか
6. "Who is it?" Dare desu ka? だれですか

GETTING MORE ACQUAINTED

Good job, you have probably been talking for a few minutes at this point. You've worked through introductions and asking questions when you need to, and maybe, you know the person's name, and you are heading the café together. Now is a good time to get to know one another just a little bit more. These questions will help you to take the conversation to a whole new level.

1. "What time is it right now?" Ima nanji desu ka? 今何時ですか
2. "Now" Ima 今
3. "Later" Ato de 後で
4. "Today" Kyou 今日

5. "Again" Mata また

6. "Want to meet" Aitai 会いたい

7. "Yesterday" Kinou 昨日

8. "Tomorrow" Ashita 明日

9. "This week" Konshuu こんしゅう

10. "Everyday" Mainichi 毎日

11. "How old are you?" Nansai desu ka? 何歳ですか

12. "Where do you live?" Doko ni sundeimasu ka? どこに住んでいますか

13. "Do you have siblings?" Kyoudai ga imasu ka? 兄弟がいますか

14. "How much does that cost?" Ikura desu ka? いくらですか

15. "What is this?" Kore wa nan desu ka? これは何ですか

16. "What is that?" Sore wa nan desu ka? それは何です

17. "What is that?" Are we nan desu ka? あれウェなんですか — you should use "kore" when something is close, "sore" when it is away from you but close to another person, and "are" when it isn't close to either one of you.

18. "Where's the toilet?" Toire wa doko desu ka?
トイレはどこですか

Here is another example of a conversation. This could be how you ask somebody how old they are in the politest way possible.

"Tomo, it looks like our hobbies are very similar. If you don't mind me asking how old are you?"

- "Tomo san watashitachi no shumi ga totemo niteirugyoudesune. Moshi sashisasae nakereba ikutsu desuka."
- 智さん、私たちの趣味がとても似ているようですね。もし差し支えなければいくつですか。

"I am 35 years old. How about you?"

- "Watashi wa san juu go sai desu. Aki san wai-kutsu desuka."
- わたしは三十五歳です。亜紀さんはいくつですか。

"I'm 35, too. Wow. So we are from the same genera-
tion."

- "Watashi mo san juu go sai desu. Sugoi. Issho
  no sedai nandesune."
- わたしも三十五歳です。すごい。一緒の世
  代なんですね。

When you are asking "ikutsu desu ka?" you are asking
them their age in the politest way possible. This is the
most common way people will ask this question.
There will be times when you hear, "nansai desu ka,"
which is simply something that is more casual and
means "what age?"

ELEVEN ANSWERS TO COMMON QUESTIONS

You've gotten to learn quite a bit about the person you
are talking with, but now. they have started asking you
questions. How are you going to respond to a lot of the
questions you have asked them? You could use some
of these.

1. "Yes" Hai はい
2. "No" Lie いいえ

3. "Not yet" mada mada まだまだ

4. "Maybe" or "I'm not sure" Kamoshiremasen かもしれません

5. "Sometimes" Tokidoki 時々

6. "Never" Zenzen 全然

7. "Always" Itsumo いつも

8. "Usually" Taitei たいてい

9. "I'm a ___" Watashi wa ___ desu 私は___です — you put anything in the blank that describes who you are.

10. "That's okay" Daijouba desu 大丈夫です

11. "That's good" ii desu いいです

There is a little difference between ii and daijoubu. If a person asks you if a person is "all right," then you would answer with daijoubu. If you find something nice or you approve of something, then you would say ii.

FIVE PHRASES FOR SPECIAL MOMENTS

What if the reason that you are talking to somebody new is that you have decided to go to a special event or celebration, such as a festival or birthday? The following are some phrases that you could use in nearly any situation you find yourself in.

1. "Be careful" Ki o tsukete 気を付けて — you could say this to a person who is getting ready to leave on a trip.

2. "Great job" Yoku dekimashita よくできました

3. "Congratulations" Omedetaou gozaimasu おめでたおうございます

4. "Happy birthday" Tanjoubi omedetou 誕生日おめでとう

5. "Cheers" Kanpai 乾杯 — you should only say this if you are actually holding a drink.

FOUR GOODBYES

You have talked for a while, but you know the conversation is coming to an end. It is important that you know how to wrap up the conversation.

6. "Well" Ja じゃ — you would use this in a sentence like, "Well, I should probably get going."

7. "Goodbye" Sayounara さようなら — you should only say this if you know you won't see them for a very long time.

8. "Well, see you" Ja, mata じゃまた — this is the more common goodbye said in Japanese.

9. "Goodnight" Oyasumi nasai おやすみなさい

Once you are ready to close the conversation, you may decide that you want to meet up again. If that be the case, then you may say something like this.

"I'd like to see you again. When are you free?"

- "Mata aitai desu. Itsu aitemasuka."
- また会いたいです。いつ空いてますか。

"I'm pretty busy this week. How about next Monday?"

- "Konshuu wa kekkou isogashii desu. Raishuu no getsuyoubi wa doudesuka."
- 今週は結構忙しいです。来週の月曜日はどうですか。

"I'm not free next week. Just let me know when you are free next month."

119

- "Raishuu wa aitemasen. Raigetsu ni aitara oshiete kudasai."
- 来週は空いてません。来月に空いたら教えてください。

"Sure, I'll send you an e-mail. See you soon."

- "Mochiron. Meeru wo okurimasu. Dewa mata aimashou."
- もちろん。メエルを送ります。出羽また会いましょう。

THREE EMERGENCY PHRASES

It is important to know what you should say in case of an emergency. Nobody wants to think about finding themselves in trouble, but it can happen. Know these phrases could save you or somebody else's life.

10. "Help me" Tasukete 助けて
11. "Please, call the police" Keisatsu o yande kudasai 警察を病んでください
12. "Please, call an ambulance" Kyuu kyuusha o yonde kudasai 救急車を呼んでください

Hopefully, you won't ever have to use these phrases, but it is always a good idea to know them.

Now that you have all of these conversation starters and sample conversations, start practicing them. Say them out loud over and over again. This will help you in memorizing them and getting used to saying Japanese words. Review these conversations as much as you can

As long as you have mastered a small number of Japanese phrases, you are doing well and getting closer to holding a conversation with a native speaker. When it comes to learning a language, you don't need to try and re-invent the wheel every time you talk to somebody new. You also don't need to come up with all the answers. Try to think about your answers to possible questions before you have a conversation so that you already know the right words. When you have a good idea as to what to expect, and you have gotten ready in advance, you will find that holding conversations with native speakers will be a lot easier. You will also feel more confident.

Chapter 7

TALKING ABOUT YOURSELF

When you are first learning Japanese, or you have an upcoming trip to Japan, there are a few words that you absolutely have to know:

1. Sumimasen
2. Arigatou
3. Konnichiwa

When you have mastered these words, then you should move onto learning your jikoshoukai. This is Japanese for "self-introduction." Basically, this is just like you would introduce yourself to people in your hometown. You would say "hello," state your name, and give them a quick introduction to who you are. In practice, there will be certain procedures and cultural differences that you have to stick to. Since you just get one chance at a good first impression, it's important that you understand how to do things correctly.

We will work through some simple introductions and look at a few cultural subtleties, and we will then go over vocab and grammar that you will be able to use when talking to your new friends.

When it comes to a self-introduction in Japanese, there are some specific orders and phrases, and this allows beginners to meet and greet in Japan.

VOCABULARY ON INTRODUCTIONS

"How do you do?" はじめまして, hajimemashite

The phrase hajimemashite can come from the verb hajimeru that means "to start." It is a shortened version of hajimete haji o-me-me ni kakarimashite or "the first time I met you." While etymologists aren't quite sure as to the actual origin of the word, hajimemashite does imply the start or doing something you have never done before. There are a lot of people who believe it to mean "Nice to meet you" or "How do you do?"

"My name is ~ " 私は〜と申します, watashi wa ~ to moshimasu

Let's break this sentence down into three parts:

1. The first word, watashi, simply means either "me" or "I." It is followed by a particle wa that gives you the topic of the sentence. In this sentence, watashi is the topic.
2. The symbol "~" represents your name.
3. To moshimasu: one meaning of this is "to be called." This gets places with the particle "to" and then conjugated to moshimasu. This is a safe choice for any situation because it is a polite phrase.

When all of this is placed together, you will have something like: "I am called..." or "My name is..."

"Please be kind to me." よろしきょねがいします, yoroshiku onegaishimasu

The final part is yoroshiku onegaishimasu. This one doesn't translate well, which is why I am adding it here. When you are using this during a self-introduction, it could mean: "Please be kind to me." Sometimes, it is translated into: "Nice to meet you." This isn't a technically correct translation even though it does give the same feeling.

We have now gone over the basics, so it is time to put the pieces of the puzzle together. In its simplest form, it would look something like this:

"How do you do? My name is ~. Please be kind to me."

はじめまして? 私は〜と申します.
よろしきょねがいします

Hajimemashite. Watashi wa ~to moshimasu. Yoroshiku onegaishimasu

Now, that wasn't so hard, was it? Make sure you practice this until it feels completely natural, so when you meet a Japanese for the first time, you can talk to them with confidence. If you are new to the Japanese language, you aren't going to need anything more.

ETIQUETTE

It is great to know the words you should say when you are introducing yourself. But, the way you say these words can either help or harm your jikoshoukai.

There are a lot of cultural differences that you need to make sure you are aware of. They tend to be very subtle and are easy to miss, but if you do miss them, they aren't going to hold it against you. If you can pay attention to these details, it will help to boost your introduction when you are meeting a Japanese person for the first time.

1. Family name and first name

    In the English language, we normally introduce ourselves by our first names or our full name. And when we do share our full name, we always say our first name first and our surname after.

    In Japan, they always introduce themselves by either their full name or just their surname. If they introduce themselves by their full name, their surname will always come first, and their first name will be second.

2. Occupation

    In the English language, if you are asked what your occupation is, you will give the name of your profession or a short summary about what you do.

    In Japan, it is normal for them to just answer with either: "I'm a salaryman," "I work for a company," or "I'm an office worker."

    If you have to introduce yourself in a business setting, you need to make sure you mention the company when you introduce yourself. It might look something like this:

    "I'm Koichi from Tofugu." Tofugu のこういちともうします. Tofugu no kouichi to moshimasu

    This takes us to our next point.

3. Don't talk a lot about yourself

Japanese people often use self-deprecation to show they are humble, but it is normally followed by something positive. Look at this:

"I might have many flaws, but I'll do my best, so please be kind to me."

至らない点が王位かもしれませんが、頑張りますので、よろしくお願いします、

Itaranai ten ga oi kamo shiremasenga, ganbarimasunode, yoroshiku o negai shimasu

You don't have to say this, but the main point is the Japanese will keep their strengths low-key.

Don't try to show off too much. You can reveal a couple of strengths, but if you start listing off everything you can do, you are going to annoy them, and you will come off as too confident.

4. Handshake versus bowing

In America, if you meet someone new, you normally shake hands.

When in Japan, you don't go for a handshake, especially if you are of lower status to the person you are talking with. In Japan, only equals will shake hands. You would be seen as rude if you were to try to shake the hand of an Emperor. You need to just bow, and you should do this before your jikoshoukai and after.

5. Keeping your hands behind your back

In Japan, if you keep your hands behind your back, you are showing importance. If you do this, it might make you look like you are full of yourself. Make sure that you keep your hands in front of you. The left hand should be on top of the right, or you can keep them by your side.

6. Never bow when talking

This is a huge no-no. Bow after you have given your self-introduction. Be sure you say "yoroshiku onegaishimasu" and bow afterward.

BUSINESS CARDS

Meishi, 名刺, or business cards are very important in

Japanese culture. Even if someone doesn't have a business, Japanese people will have personal meishi made. Here is some meishi etiquette that you need to know:

- You meishi should be in a case. You can purchase carrying cases for your business cards at most department stores in Japan or online. If, by chance, you don't have a case, place a meishi you have received in your wallet or purse. Don't put them in a pocket.

- Hold it with both hands. Place the card toward the person you are giving it to. Use both of your hands to hold the top edge. If you are handed a card, use both hands to accept it. Try your best to make sure the words on the card are not covered by your hands. Japanese people view the meishi as the person's face who is giving it to you. You wouldn't want to cover up your face or theirs.

- If the meishis are presented at the same time, you should present with your right hand and accept it with the left.

- Read the meishi that you get. Make sure that you read the card before you put it away. Be sure you act interested in what their profession is. Act impressed by their job title.

- When you are exchanging meishi with a group of people, hand the oldest person the meishi first.

- Always treat the meishi with complete respect. Make sure that you use common sense and treat all of the meishis you receive like they were a gift. Never place them in a pocket or toss them on a table, and don't ever, EVER write on them.

PASTIMES AND HOBBIES

Hobbies are a big part of the Japanese lifestyle. Students in secondary education and beyond take their extracurricular activities seriously, sometimes more serious than regular schoolwork, and this continues throughout their life. If there is a hobby you enjoy that you consider as your "thing," you should share it. Even if you don't think your interests would be considered hobbies, it is a good idea to share them. This will help people to understand you.

- "I'm not good at doing ___." Watashi wa ___ suru koto ga nigatedesu
  私は___することが苦手です
- "I'm good at ___." Watashi wa ___ ga tokui kuidesu 私は___が得意杭です
- "My hobby is to do ___." ___ suru koto ga shumidesu ___ することが趣味です

FUTURE PLANS

What are your plans for the future? What is your dream job? What is something that you would like to learn? What are you going to have for lunch tomorrow? You will be able to answer these questions, and more, once you have read through these sentences.

An important note about grammar: the noun tsumori つもり is commonly used to let a person know what you are planning on doing. This is most commonly used for things that you have already decided on. It is a definite. You should not use this in times when you might be thinking about something but haven't made up your mind.

- "I'm thinking about doing _." __Yo to kangaete imasu __ようと考えています
- "I'd like to do _." _ shitai to omotte imasu _ したいと思っています
- "I'm thinking about doing _." _ tsumoridesu _つもりです
- "My object is _." Watashi no mokuhyo wa _ desu 私の目標は__です
- "I'd like to challenge _." _ Ni chosen shitai to omotte imasu __に挑戦したいと思っています

Now, you know how to share an amazing jikoshoukai. Start putting everything together and always remember the cultural differences. Make sure you practice it until it all becomes second nature to you. When you are armed with a great introduction, you are ready to begin a relationship the best way possible.

Chapter 8

WHICH WAY DO I GO?

When trying to travel cheap in Japan, you don't want to get lost and be forced to take a cab that will cost you a fortune. Let's talk about the basics of getting and giving directions, so you will be able to find your way around without any problems.

ASKING DIRECTIONS

Let's begin with the most basic question that can be used for any occasion:

"Excuse me. Where is…?" Sumimasen. ~wa doko desu ka?

If you need to be a bit fancier and specifically asking somebody how to get to a specific place, you could say:

"Excuse me. How do I get to...?" Sumimasen. ~ni wa doyatte ikimasu ka?

RECEIVING AND GIVING DIRECTIONS

There are several expressions that someone might use, but there are some sentence patterns and keywords that will help you in most situations. Let's begin with some basic sentences:

- "Please turn left at...", ~ de hidari ni magatte kudasai
- "Please turn right at...", ~ de migi ni magatte kudasai
- "Please go straight (until)" (~made) massugu itte kudasai

The words that you need to know would be hidari for left, migi for right, massugu for straight. It might be helpful to know the verbs magarimasu for turn and ikimasu for go.

In the sentences above, the verbs are expressed in what is called the te-form. This is relevant when you are giving or getting directions since the verb form could be used for requests and commands.

You can do this by just removing kudasai from the sentences above and then just saying the phrases one after another. If you add kudasai at the end of the sentence, the whole sentence turns into a polite command. This is a lot like when adding please to the end of an English sentence. The result could look like:

"Please **go straight**, then **turn left at** the traffic lights."

Massugu itte, shingo **de hidari ni magatte** kudasai

You can string together as many phrases as you want, as long as the verb is expressed in the te-form.

Look at these phrases that you might hear every now and then:

"Please leave through this exit." Kono deguchi wo dete kudasai

"Please enter the station." Eki ni haitte kudasai

"Please cross the road." Doro wo satatte kudasai

You have everything you need to understand all sorts of directions like this.

"Please leave through this exit, turn right, go straight until the intersection, cross the road, enter the station, and turn left."

Kono deguchi wo dete migi ni magatte, kosaten made massugu itte, doro wo watatte, eki ni haitte, hidari ni magatte kudasai.

USING LANDMARKS TO COUNT

Even though the phrases above will cover the basics, the directions to a certain location won't involve turning at a landmark, such as an intersection, but it might require you to turn at another intersection down the road.

Landmarks and intersections get counted using the banme counter. If the word banme comes after a number, that number turns into an ordinal number, so number one turns into the word "first," two would be "second," etc. This gets connected to an object or place using a particle "no." Look at these examples:

"The first intersection" Ichi banme no kosaten

"The second set of traffic lights" Ni banme no shingo

"The third corner" San banme no kado

If used in sentences, these are just added into any of these phrases.

"Please turn left at the fourth intersection." Yon banme no kosaten de hidari ni magatte kudasai

"Please go straight, then turn right at the fifth set of traffic lights." Massugu itte, go banme no shingo de migi ni magatte kudasai

What if they talk too fast?

It doesn't matter if you are new to Japanese or you have spoken it for a long time, there are going to be times when you just don't follow what the person is trying to tell you. In these situations, these phrases can help you out:

"Sorry, would you please speak a little slower?" Sumimasen, mo chotto yukkuri hanashite kudasai

"Sorry, would you repeat that, please?" Sumimasen, mo ichi do onegaishimasu

Chapter 9

HOW MUCH IS THAT?

If the old saying "money makes the world go round" is true, it usually does so in silence. We all love having money, but we don't want to talk about it. Japan isn't an exception, but the Japanese vocabulary dealing with money is very expansive and amazingly complex. It deserves to be looked at a bit closer.

Money is usually called okane (お金). The prefix "o" gets rid of the taboo nature that money is bad. If you forget and end up saying something along the lines of "kane ga hoshii" or "I want money" (金が欲しい), the money you have asked for will be thought of as "dirty" money, or it wasn't earned.

The character that is usually found at the end of words to talk about different money transactions is "kin."

Sometimes, this is used to a person's detriment, like with the words fine or bakkin (罰金). You might incur a fee, such as an "admission fee" or nyukaikin (入会金), an "entrance fee" to get into a school or nyugakukin (入学金), "deposit" or shikikin (敷金), and "key money" or reikin (礼金). The latter two are needed if you plan on renting an apartment in Japan.

There are some expressions within the money family that refer to money that is coming in instead of money that is going out. Pension or nenkin (年金) is great to have for a rainy day. There are different kinds of financial support for students going to school like scholarships or shogakukins (諸学気), subsidies or hojokin (補助金), and grant-in-aid or joseikin (助成金).

Another entry for the Japanese money lexicon is ryo or 料 as is used in the word fee or ryokin (料金). The most annoying is the handling fee or tesuryo (手数料) that happens with the tiniest act. If you are traveling on a toll road, you will encounter a toll or tsukoryo (通行料). This is only peanuts when you compare it to other fees that might be waiting on you later in life, like a marriage brokerage or kekkon chukairyo

(結婚仲介料) and consolation money or isharyo (慰謝料). This is what we would consider as palimony. Another word that could be used during breakups due to adultery is alimony or tegirekin (手切れ金).

Other expenses are expressed by using the character for fee or hi (費). Some of these might include maintenance costs or ijihi (維持費), medical expenses or iryohi (医療費), education expenses or kyoikuhi (教育費), transportation costs or kotsuhi (交通費), and living expenses or seikatsuhi (生活費). When it isn't in your best interest to divulge what you spent money on, you could always clump it under various expenses or shokeihi (諸経費).

Just like hi, ryo and kin are used for charges and fees. You might find words like participation fee or sankahi (参加費) and annual membership fees or nenkaihi (年会費). If you get invited to a party where they have a system that requires a participation or membership fee or kaihisei (会費制), make sure you bring money because you will be expected to pay this.

One of the few words where 費 isn't about losses is a scientist's beloved kakenhi (科研費), which is short for kagaku kenkyuhi josei jigyo (科学研究費助成事業). This is a grant that is funded by the government. The word for general research funding is kenkyuhi (研究費).

Another good word to know is rent or chin (賃). You will see this in two terms: fare you pay for passengers or freight or unchin (運賃) and rent or yachin (家賃). It is normally used when talking about wages or income, like pay raise or chin-age (賃上げ) or the unpleasant pay cut or chingin katto (賃金カット).

When talking about getting money for work, another character is kyu (給), like for pay/salary or kyuryo (給料). Some types of payments might include daily pay or nikkyu (日給), monthly pay or gekkyu (月給), and hourly payment or jikyu (時給). There is also annual income or nenshu (年収) and daily pay or nitto (日東). If an abstract language is needed, people will use words like bonus or bonasu (ボーナス), year-end allowance or nenmatsu teate (年末手当), allowance or teate (手当), or remuneration or hoshu (報酬).

When talking about exchanging something, using shi-ro or dai (代) will be helpful. You can find it in expressions such as room charge or heyadai (部屋代), drinking money, tip or sakadai or sakashiro (酒代), car charge or kurumadai (車代), and room charge or heyadai (部屋代).

The most taboo terms to use when talking about money would be words like monthly tuition fee or gessha (月謝) that actually translates into "monthly gratitude," along with celebration or o-iwai (お祝い) and gratitude or o-rei (お礼). These are expressions that you will read when envelopes that have larger and smaller amounts change hands.

BANKING AND MONEY PHRASES

When you visit Japan, it could be very expensive for you, so you have to have a decent understanding of Japanese banking and money phrases. It doesn't matter if you are moving to Japan permanently or just going for a visit; the best way to make sure you don't spend more than you should is to become familiar with all of these different words.

- "traveler's checks," 寅平ラウズチェック, tor-aberazu chekku
- "exchange rate," 為替れと, kawasere-to
- "bank," 番組, ginko
- "money," お金, o-kane

The Japanese monetary system uses yens. It is always a good idea to exchange your currency before traveling. The money exchange is the primary need for anyone traveling to a foreign country. The following conversation is a traveler exchanging their U.S. dollars for yen.

Robert: "What is the exchange rate today?" Kyo noka-wase reto wa ikura desu ka.

Teller: "Today's exchange rate is 122 yen for one US dollar." Kyo no kawase reto wa ichi-doru hyaku-niju-ni-en desu.

Robert: "I would like to exchange $100." Hyaku-doru ryogae shitai n-desu ga.

The people who live in Japan rarely use checks. So, if you are planning on moving to Japan, you will probably open a savings account instead of a checking account.

When it comes to banking needs in Japan, these are some phrases that you may want to familiarize yourself with.

- "I would like to open a savings account." "Futsu yoking koza o hirakitai n-desu ga."
- "I'd like to cash this traveler's check." "Kono toraberazu chekku o genkin ni shitai n-desu ga."
- "Do you have any branches in the U.S.?" "Amerika ni wa shiten ga arimasu ka."
- "How many branches do you have?" "Shiten wa ikutsu arimasu ka."
- "How much can I change?" "Ikura kaeraremasu ka."
- "Where can I change money?" "Doko de okane wo kaemasu ka."
- "I want to buy some yen." "Ryougae shitai desu."

147

- "I want to change a dollar for yen." "Dollar en wo kankin shitai desu."
- "Let's go shopping!" "Kaimono ni ikou yo."
- "When does the store open?" "Mise ha nanji kara desu ka."
- "When does the store close?" "Mise ha nanji made desu ka."

JAPANESE SHOPPING VOCABULARY

You should have a working vocabulary to get cultural experience when you are traveling. When you go shopping in Japan, you get treated like a God. The Japanese provide their shoppers with some of the best services in the world. Store hours are normally between 10 AM and 11 PM. Most shops don't open until later in the morning. The earliest will be 9 AM, and stores are usually open very late, usually until midnight. Rather than getting up early, take time to relax and enjoy your breakfast. Whether you are shopping for souvenirs, food, or clothes, you can use these phrases to help you:

- "How much?" "Ikura?"

- "What are you looking for?" "Nani o o-sagashi desu ka."
- "Welcome!" "Irasshaimase!"
- "No, thank you." "Ie, ii desu."
- "I like that one over there." "Are ga ii desu."
- "There is a problem with the change." "Otsuri ga chigaimasu."
- "It's a gift." "Okurimono desu."
- "Can you deliver to my hotel?" "Watashi no hotel ni haisou shite moraimasu ka?"
- "I'll come back." "Mata kimasu."
- "I'll think about it." "Kangaemasu."
- "What is the cost of everything?" "Zenbu de ikura desu ka."
- "I'll take one of each." "Hitorizutsu wo kudasai."
- "I'll take this one." "Kore wo kudasai."
- "Is it made in Japan?" "Nihon san desu ka."
- "Where does it come from?" "Doko no kuni desu ka."
- "Which one is better?" "Dochi ga ii to omou?"
- "This is better this way." "Kono hou ga ii yo."
- "How's this?" "Kore ha hou desu ka."

- "This is great." "Kore ha suteki."
- "It's perfect." "Pittari desu."
- "I'm buying for a friend." "Tomodashi ni ageru tsumori desu."
- "It's long." "Nagai."
- "It's a bit tight." "Chotto kitsui."
- "It's too small for me." "Ookisugiru."
- "May I try it on?" "Kite mite mo ii desu ka."
- "Do you have this sweater in red?" "Kono seta no aka ha arimasu ka."
- "Do you have this shirt in a bigger size?" "Kono shirt no ookii size ha arimasu ka."
- "Do you have it in a smaller size?" "Kore no chisai size ha arimasu ka."
- "That's cheap." "Yasui."
- "That's too much." "Takasugiru."
- "That's expensive!" "Takai."
- "How much is this?" "Kore ha ikura desu ka."
- "Not just yet." "Mada kekkou desu."
- "I'm just looking." "Mite iru dake desu."
- "I'm looking for a black leather bag." "Kuro-kawa no bag wo sagashiteimasu."

- "The women's clothing is on the 7th floor." "Josei na fuku ha nana kai desu."
- "Where's the clothes department?" "Fuku uri-ba ha doko desu ka."
- "It's on the third floor." "San kai desu."
- "Where's the shoe department?" "Kutsu uriba ha doko desu ka."

When you are shopping in Japan, you don't have to spend a lot of money. There are several 100 yen shops throughout Japan where you can get things for less. Their most popular 100 yen shop chain is Daiso.

You can use the following words in many shopping situations:

- "bag" kaban
- "small" chiisai desu
- "price" genka
- "large, tall, big" okii desu
- "expensive" takai
- "credit card" kurejitto kado
- "cash" genkin
- "money" o-kane

WHERE TO SHOP

Most people think about Japan as being the shopping mecca of the world. There are a lot of different stores where you can find traditional products, the latest gadgets, as well as antiques. The first thing you need for a successful shopping trip is to know exactly where the best shops are located. If you need to find a certain store, these terms might help:

- "grocery store" kanbutsuya
- "supermarket" sopamaketto
- "department store" depato
- "discount store" disukauntosutoa
- "convenience store" konbini

Shopping for Groceries

There are many stores in Japan that carry groceries. These range from small stores that are owned by families to large supermarket chains. The larger cities even have Costcos. You might find these words helpful when you shop for food:

- "bread: pan"
- "fruit: kudamono"
- "vegetables: yasai"
- "eggs: tamago"
- "fish: sakana"
- "chicken: toriniku"
- "pork: butaniku"
- "meat: niku"
- "uncooked rice: o-kome"
- "wine: wain"
- "beer: biru"
- "milk: gyunyu"
- "coffee: kohi"

While you are shopping in a supermarket for whatever you might need, the cashier might ask you:

- "Would you like chopsticks?" ashi go orio desu ka
- "Would you like a plastic bag?" furo ga oria desu ka

You could answer: "Yes, please / thanks" Hai, onegai shimasu

Nouns in Japanese don't have either a plural or singular distinction. They aren't preceded by either the or a. You might be wondering how a Japanese person will know if you want just one fish or multiples when you order fish or sakana. The only way they will know is if they guess or ask you how many.

Shopping for Clothes

Most clothes are sold at either discount stores or disukauntosutoa or department stores or depato. These phrases could help you when you are shopping for clothes.

- "When will the sale start?" "Scru wa itsu kara desu ka."

- "May I return this item?" "Kore o henpin shite mo ii desu ka."

- "May I pay by credit card?" "Kurejitto kado de haratte moii desu ka."

- "This watch is expensive." "Kono tokei wa takai desu."

- "I would like to purchase this skirt." "Kono sukaato o kudasai."

- "How much is this shirt?" "Kono shatsu wa ikura desu ka."

- "This one, please." "Kore o onegai shimasu."

- "I'll take this one." "Kore o kudasai."

- "Do you have this in size large?" "Kore no eru-saizu wa arimasu ka."

- "This one is too big." "Kore wa okisugimasu."

- "This one is too small." "Kore wa chisasugi-masu."

- "Where is the fitting room?" "Shichakushitsu wa doko desu ka."

- "May I try it on?" "Kite mite no ii desu ka."

- "I like that one over there." "Are ga ii desu."

- "How about this one?" "Kore wa ikaga desu ka."

- "I am looking for a black dress." "Kuroi doresu o sagashite imasu."

A lot of the department stores will have discount sales during the main gift-giving seasons: O'chugen, which is in June and July, and O'seibo, during December and January.

- "shoe" kutsu
- "jacket" jaketto
- "sweater" scta
- "pants" zubon
- "jeans" jinzu
- "suit" sutsu
- "blouse" burausu
- "shirt" shatsu
- "hat" boshi
- "dress" wanpisu

Colors

These are some of the most common colors used in Japanese. Some colors are expressed as nouns, while others are expressed by adjectives.

- "green" midori
- "yellow" kiiroi desu
- "white" shiroi desu
- "red" akai desu
- "blue" aoi desu
- "black" kuroi desu

Japan is a country where you will find excellent service. You will likely find it extremely easy to go shopping in large stores, as well as the discount stores. You might find some difficulty in restaurants, but you should still have a very enjoyable experience.

Chapter 10

VACATIONS WITH EASE

Do you absolutely have to speak Japanese when you travel to Japan? No. You can visit Japan without knowing any of these phrases and words and have a wonderful time. Language barriers are just a common myth that doesn't need to get in your way.

Most travelers are very surprised by how easy it is to get around Japan without speaking a word of Japanese. Most people come back with wonderful stories about how much fun they had.

THE ESSENTIAL PHRASES AND WORDS

Other than the fact that it is a fascinating and rich language, learning a couple of phrases or words could help you endear yourself to the Japanese people you encounter while traveling in this beautiful land.

With all the cheap and, sometimes, free happenings close to Tokyo, you might find yourself navigating the confusing bus, subway, and train networks.

These people are very appreciative of visitors that take time to learn some of their languages, and when you try them out, chances are, you are going to be greeted with some "aahs" and "oohs" of encouragement.

To help you on your trip, we have found the most helpful Japanese phrases and words for your travels through Japan. Don't worry about pronouncing everything correctly. Japanese isn't a tonal language like most languages in Asia, and pronouncing these phrases and words is a lot easier than you might think.

- "Where is the...?" ～はどこですか？, ~wa doko desu ka?

  It is very useful to know how to ask "Where is the...?" This is helpful even if you don't know the answer since when you have asked, people could still point to where you need to go, or they might even walk you to where you want to go. All you have to do is fill in the blank with where you want to go before you ask the question. So you would say "… wa doko desu ka?"

- "I would like…, please."
  〜おください、よろしくおねがいします, 〜
  o kudasai, yoroshiku onegaishimasu.

This is a useful sentence that could help you in many situations, like in stores, restaurants, and several other occasions that you might encounter on your travels. All you have to do is fill in the blank with what you need. You could learn some essential needs such as sake, beer (biiru), or water (mizu).

- "Excuse me." すみません, sumimasen

This is an important phrase in all languages, and Japanese is no exception. You might find that you use this one quite often, and it would be best to learn it. It is very useful as you can use it to apologize and to get someone's attention.

- "Hello." こんにちわ, konnichiwa

Everyone needs to know how to say hello in any language, and you might have heard kon-nichiwa before. It is normally used during day-time hours, as there are other phrases for good evening (ohayou gozaimasu) and good morn-ing (konbanwa). If you are just beginning to learn the language, it is fine to keep things simple. If you can learn konnichiwa, it is fine to use it all day long.

- "Thank you." ありがとうございます, ariga-tou gozaimasu

You will find yourself saying "thank you" many times. The "u" at the end is barely pronounced and is almost silent. You could get by with just saying arigatou, which is the informal way of saying "thank you." Since being super polite is the key in Japan, you should say arigatou gozaimasu, so you don't offend anyone.

FINDING YOUR DESTINATION

Once you get into Japan, the first thing you have to do is know where you are going. Here are some simple ways to ask questions:

- "How do I get to…?"
  どうやって〜にいきますか？, douyatte ～ ni ikimasu ka?
- "Where is the bus to…?"
  〜ゆきのばすはどこですか？, ～yuki   no basu wa doko desu ka?
- "Where is the train to…?"
  〜ゆきのでんしゃはどこですか？, ～yuki no densha wa doko desu ka?

It isn't any use to ask the question if you can't understand what they tell you. It will be impossible to cover every expression that someone could use to give you direction, but here are a few phrases or words that you might hear:

- "Toward…", 〜ほうめん, ～homen
- "Bound for…", 〜ゆき, ～yuki
- "The… line," 〜せん, ～sen

- "Platform number...", 〜ばんせん, ~ban sen
- "Get off at...", 〜でおります, ~de orimasu
- "Change buses at...", 〜でのりかえて, de norikaete
- "Change trains at...", 〜でのりかえます, de norikaemasu
- "Transfer," のりかえ, norikae
- "To take...", 〜のって, ~notte
- "To ride...", 〜のります, ~norimasu

If you are in Shibuya, and you asked somebody directions on how to get to the city Roppongi, they might answer with the following:

"Please take the Yamanote line toward Shinagawa, then change to the Hibiya line at Ebisu."

やまのてせんをしながわほうめんいのって、えび
すでひびやせんにのりかえてください

"Yamanote-sen wo shinagawa homen ni note, ebisu de hibiya-sen ni norikaete kudasai."

Directions that are complicated might be a little bit of a problem, but if you can't understand somebody, just ask them to say it again slowly. Just say "sumimasen, mo chotto yukkuri onegaishimasu," and focus on words such as line names or station names. Listen for words like "homen" and "norikae."

ASKING FOR INFORMATION

When you are walking around Japan, there might be a good chance that you want to know how much it is going to cost you to take a bus or train and how long the trip will be. Here are some questions you can ask:

- "How long does it take to go to…?", 　〜までわどれくらいかかりますか？, 　~made wa dore kurai kakarimasu ka?
- "How much does it cost to go to…?", 　〜までわいくらですか？, ~made wa ikura desu ka?

Their answers might be straightforward, but you will need to know numbers. They will use the "en" for yen, and the "jikan" or "fun" for hours and minutes.

PURCHASING TICKETS

When you take a bus in Japan, you just pay as you get off or on the bus, but trains require you to purchase a ticket. The common word that is used when talking about train tickets is "kippu," but if it is easier for you to remember, you can also use "chiketto." When asking somebody where you can purchase a ticket, you could say:

"Where can I buy a ticket?"
きっぷはどこでかえますか？, kippu wa doko de kaemasu ka?

You have to be careful at train stations with many train lines run by various companies. Most of the time, tickets for one line isn't going to work with another. You have to make sure that you use the correct ticket machine. These machines are well-marked, but not all the time. You have to be careful. If you aren't sure, just ask somebody. You could make the question above more specific by adding the "sen," or something like this:

"Where can I buy a ticket for the … line?"
〜せんおきっぷはどこでかえますか？, ~sen no kippu wa doko de kaemasu ka?

By the way, the word "sen" has multiple meanings. It might be referring to the train line, the platform number, or the train company. You just need to be sure you are buying tickets for the correct company unless you are purchasing tickets for the bullet train or express that has reserved seating because the line isn't specific.

MAKE SURE YOU GET ON THE CORRECT BUS OR TRAIN

Before you actually get on a bus or train, you could save yourself some time by making sure you aren't getting on something that is going to take you in the complete opposite direction. You could ask another traveler, the station attendant, or the bus driver these questions:

- "Does this train stop at…?",
  このでんしゃは〜のともりますか？, kono densha wa ~ ni tomarimasu ka?

- "Does this bus stop at...?",
  このばすは〜にとまりますか？, kono basu wa ~ ni tomarimasu ka?
- "Is this the train to...?",
  これは〜ゆきのべんしゃですか？, kore wa ~ yuki no densha desu ka?
- "Is this the bus to...?"
  これは〜ゆきのばすですか？, kore wa ~ yuki no basu desu ka?

You could just take a taxi. These are fairly easy to understand since the driver only has one question to ask you, so your answer only needs to be the landmark or address of the place you are going. Just be aware that taxis in Japan aren't cheap in Tokyo. If you don't want to have to sell a body part once you reach your destination, you should ask the driver something like this:

"I want to go to... but how much will it cost?"
〜にいきたいですが、いくらくらいかかりますか？, ~ ni ikitai desu ga, kiura kurai kakarimasu ka?

Don't expect them to answer you precisely, but it might give you a ballpark figure as to whether or not you can afford it and if you should find a cheaper ride.

MAKING YOUR HOTEL EXPERIENCE BETTER

If you have ever been confused about services offered or where to find something at a hotel in a foreign country, read on to find some Japanese phrases that will make your experience easier and better while visiting Japan.

- "Room service, please." るむさびす、おねがいします, rumu sabisu, onegai shimasu
- "Taxi, please." たくし、おねがいします, takushi, onegai shimasu
- "Key, please." かぎ、おねがいします, kagi, onegai shimasu.

You would use this when you want to receive your key or leave your key.

- "Check out, please."
  ちぇっくあうと、おねがいします, chekku
  auto, onegai shimasu
- "..., please." 〜おねがいします, ~ onegai
  shimasu

Use this when you need to ask for something at the front desk

- "Check-in, please."
  ちぇっくいん、おねがいします, chekku in,
  onegai shimasu

Here are some questions you might need to ask:

- "Do you have Wi-Fi?"
  うぃふぃはありますか？, Wi-Fi wa, arimasuka?
- "Do you have the password?"
  ぱすわどはありますか？, pasuwado wa, arimasuka?
- "Do you have a map?"
  ちずはありますか？, chizu wa arimasuka?

- "Is there an ATM?" ATM はありますか？, ATM wa, arimasuka?

- "Do you have a safe?"
  きんこはありますか？, kinko wa arimasuka?

- "Do you have an iron?"
  あいろんはありますか？, airon wa arimasuka?

- "Where is the beauty salon?"
  えすてはどこですか？, esute wa, doko desuka?

- "Where is the gym?" じむはどこですか？, jimu wa, doko desuka?

- "Where is the nearest station?"
  いちばんちかいえきはどこですか？,
  ichiban chikai eki wa doko desuka?

- "Where is the nearest supermarket?"
  いちばんちかいすぱはどこですか？,
  ichiban chikai, supa wa, doko desuka?

- "Where is the nearest sushi restaurant?"
  いちばんちかいすしやはどこですか？,
  ichiban chikai sushiya wa, doko desuka?

- "What time is breakfast?"
  ちょしょくはなんじですか？, choshoku wa nanji desuka?

- "Can you change money?"
  りょがえはできますか？, ryogae wa, deki-masuka?

- "Can you do room service?"
  るむさびすはできますか？, rumu sabisu wa, dekimasuka?

- "Can you do massages?"
  まっさじはできますか？, massaji wa, deki-masuka?

If you need help with something, you could say something like:

- "I can't use the Wi-Fi." Wi-Fi
  がつかえません, Wi-Fi ga tsukaemasen

- "I can't use the air conditioner."
  えあこんがつかえません, eakon go tsukae-masen

- "I can't use the safe." きんこがつかえません,
  kinko ga tsukaemasen

- "I can't use the shower."
  しゃわごつかえません, shawa ga tsukae-masen

When you are checking out, say something like:

- "Can I leave my bags here?"
  にもつはあずけられますか？, nimotsu wa azuke raremasuka?

If you forgot something in your room:

- "I forgot my shaver."
  ひげそりをわすれました, higesori wo wasure mashita
- "I forgot my cell phone."
  けたいをわすれました, ketai wo wasure ma-shita
- "I forgot my camera."
  かめらをわすれました, camera wo wasure mashita

After you have checked into the hotel, the receptionist is going to give you the key and tell you which room you are in. Some hotels won't have room number four or nine. Four or "shi" means "death," while nine or "ku" means "pain."

- "You are in room number two."
  あなとのおへやはにごうしつです, anata no o heya wa ni goshitsu desu
- "The key number." **かぎのばんごう**, kagi no bango
- "The key." **かご**, kagi

You might want to know where to find these things:

- "Where do you serve breakfast?"
  ちょうしょくはどこでたべますか？ chosho ku wa doko de tabemasu ka?
- "Where is the restaurant?"
  レストラン/しょくどうはどこですか？ resu toran/ shokudo wa doko desu ka?
- "Where is the swimming pool?"
  プールはどこですか？, puru wa doko desu ka?
- "Where is the elevator?"
  エレベーターはどこですか？, erebeta wa doko desu ka?

You might also need to know:

- "When do you serve breakfast?"
  ちょうしょくはなんじですか？, choshoku
  wa nanji desu ka?
- "Do I pay now or later?"
  いまはらいましょうこそれともあとで？,
  ima haraimasho ka soretomo atode?
- "At what time do I need to check out of the
  room?"
  チェックアウトはなんじうですか？,
  chekku auto wa nanji desu ka?

If you find that there are things missing from your
room, here are some phrases you could use:

- "I need an extra blanket."
  もうがもういちまいひつようです, mofu ga
  mo ichi mai hitsuyo desu.
- "I need more toilet paper."
  トイレットペーパーがひつようです, poiret-
  to pepa ga hitsuyo desu.

- "I need more soap."

  せっけんがひつとうです, sekken ga hitsuyo desu

- "I need more towels." タオルがひつよです, taoru ga hitsuyo desu.

These phrases or words might also be useful:

- "unacceptable," きにいらあい, kini iranai
- "broken," こわれる, kowareru
- "the light," あかり, akari
- "the water," みず, mizu
- "hot," あつい, atsui
- "cold," さむい, samui
- "clean," きれい, kirei
- "noisy," うるさい, urusai
- "dirty," きたない, kitanai
- "The heater is broken."

  だんぼうがこわれています, danbo ga kowarete imasu

- "The heater," だんぼう, danbo
- "The air conditioning," れうぼう, rebo
- "A double bed," ダブルベッド, daburu beddo

Chapter 11

TIPS FOR LEARNING QUICKLY

Japanese is said to be one of the hardest languages for people to learn along with Cantonese, Mandarin, Korean, and Arabic.

Japanese uses a sentence structure called Subject-Object-Verb or SOV, while the English language is a Subject-Verb-Object or SVO language. If you were to try to translate Japanese into English, you would sound like Yoda; you would.

Unlike the Romance or English languages, there are three lexical systems to the Japanese language: kanji, katakana, and hiragana. Plus, there are various tenses for the levels of informality and humbleness. Japanese is a very contextual language that was built on hints instead of direct communication.

How much fun does that sound? Use these tips to help you learn this language quickly:

1. Visit Japan but leave the city

    It doesn't matter how many people you talk to, the movies you watch, or the books you read, you aren't going to be able to experience Japan until you are there in person. Your ability to read and speak will get so much better and a lot faster. Don't forget to continue using them when you go back home. Rather than just acting like a tourist, volunteer at a farm, or stay at a person's home. The larger cities are full of Japanese people who like practicing their English-speaking skills on you, so you need to get as far away from them as possible. This is the best way to get the most out of your Japan trip in a short amount of time. Remember to sing some karaoke and have loads of fun.

2. Learn sound effects and tongue twisters

    Tongue twisters will make you look at Japanese in different ways; they are also instant conversations starters. Unlike English, sound effects are usually only found in cartoons and comic books; here, sound effects are part of their daily speech. You might sound more natural if you could learn them. A Japanese person might say "peko peko" to describe their stomach growling. If they add "desu" to the end of the phrase, it will change into "I am hungry." There are four different ways to describe the sound of rain in Japanese. They can even describe silence. "Hayakuchi kotoba" is the Japanese word for "tongue twister," which translates into "fast mouth words."

3. Be careful with immersion programs

Immersing yourself in the country is a great way to learn a language, but this is more for advanced students who need to help their fluency. You could still get a good start.

Inside the United States, there are some summer camps and immersion programs for college students and children but always do some research before you jump into the pool. Some programs won't allow anyone to speak in English, and they might force you to speak Japanese whatever your level might be. Some programs ignore the fact that adult beginners are past the learning stage.

You should ask yourself: "How much will I get out of a university-level course that is done totally in Japanese if I am not fluent yet?" You can't expect to cram the information so you can catch up to a higher level.

4. Find a conversation partner when you start

You don't have to pay a lot for this. Most Japanese people will usually barter for English lessons. Listening to another person and listening to yourself will help enforce the right pronunciation while you are urging them to make corrections to your speech when needed. The rewards come from the fact that you are teaching your brain how to think in Japanese.

Reading conversations in a textbook will always be predictable, and no one actually talks like that. When you teach Japanese to yourself, you aren't giving yourself an opportunity to practice the conversation. There are lots of groups that meet pretty much anywhere, and you could always check with the local community centers and schools for any opportunity.

5. Sing in Japanese while following the lyrics

Following lyrics can help you recognize kanji and kana. It can help you hear how Japanese really sounds, along with increasing your reading speeds. This is very important since karaoke is the unofficial national sport in Japan. People in Japan love it when a tourist can sing their songs, so practice every chance you get. Karaoke groups are great ways to make friends.

6. Watch all the movies and cartoons, and listen to all the music you want

The Japanese culture has become more popular with young people, thanks to manga, anime, and Japanese music. Most fans like to read even though they don't understand what is going on, so they try to translate the lyrics word for word.

Even though this is a great way to learn their slang and grammar patterns, it can teach you a vocabulary that is useless in normal daily speech. You might be able to say words for butterfly, swallowtail, unforgivable, eternity, tears, embrace, overflowing, and heartbeat, but you are going to be in a heap of trouble if you are stuck in Tokyo without knowing the words for post office, right, left, turn, train line, airport, staircase, and bank.

7.   Buy some quality materials

If you decide to take Japanese while in school, the textbook has been chosen for you, but a bad textbook could hinder you from learning well. I did have a Japanese teacher who told us that some of the terms in our textbook were outdated. What good is it to have a book that is outdated? You aren't going to learn anything.

You have all kinds of choices if you are looking for materials for learning Japanese. Textbooks are more like guidelines, and it all depends on your learning style.

Find a good dictionary that has hiragana for all the kanji, kanji, and the English definition for it. You don't need to worry about kanji cards or a dictionary until later on in your studies. You can also find books on pop culture, culture dictionaries, and slang Japanese.

8. If it's hard, don't skip it

It might be easy to think that you will go back to a chapter you skipped, but truthfully, you won't. The first parts are always about particles, telling time, and family titles. Conversations within the textbook will use family and time as topics, but mastering particles will take a lot longer than it should. You have to learn how to conjugate adjectives. Never move to the next lesson until you are able to do it while you sleep.

9. Never study without supervision

Even though it is easy to teach yourself the syllabaries of katakana and hiragana, the stroke order is usually discarded by people just learning the language. When you are learning how to write your letters in English, it is another character quirk. With the Japanese people, they will just assume you were just too lazy to learn it the right way. The same assumption could be attributed if you don't know how to hold chopsticks the right way.

There is a huge difference between finishing a pen stroke with a swoosh or a sudden stop. Stroke order is essential when learning the kanji basics. Never skip this part.

Chapter 12

THINGS YOU SHOULD AVOID SAYING

Japan is the top tourist destination every year. Japan attracts millions of people from all over the world who want to visit shrines, temples, and castles. They want to take part in the colorful and vibrant spring, winter, autumn, and summer festivals the world has to offer. You can see picturesque and stunning waterscapes and landscapes. You could get to experience the bustling nightlife, the renowned hot springs or therapeutic onsen, solemn temple stays, and high-tech Japanese toilets. You can feast on all their mouthwatering cuisine like sushi and ramen.

Since this is a foreign country that has culture and history that you might not be familiar with and a language that you can't speak, you could commit several etiquette fails that could offend these people. Many people don't realize that translating words and phrases from an app or dictionary won't give them what they want to say.

If you don't want to be offensive or rude to a Japanese person when you visit this country, here are some tips that could help you out:

- When you get a compliment, don't thank the person

    If a Japanese person compliments you, as they tell you that you look great in your new dress or your presentation was great, you shouldn't say "arigatou gozaimasu." This is the same thing as "thank you" in the English language. Japanese people don't thank others when getting a compliment. They use a more modest response. In order to show your appreciation for a compliment, you need to say either "zenzen" or "iie." This roughly translates into English as "no, not at all."

- Never say "sayonara" when telling friends or family goodbye.

If you look up a translation for "goodbye" in Google, it is going to give you the word "sayonara." When you use "sayonara" to tell somebody goodbye, and you know you are going to see them the next day or in a few weeks or days, it is wrong.

Japanese only use "sayonara" when they won't see someone they know for a very long time. You can use "sayonara" to bid goodbye to your new friend whom you just met at the hostel you were staying in as you probably won't see them again for a very long time.

If you would like a casual way to say goodbye to someone you will see tomorrow, you can use either "ja mata" or "ja nee." Both of these translate to "see you again" or "see you." These terms get used daily by Japanese people at school or work when they say goodbye to classmates or coworkers whom they are going to see the very next day.

189

- When people offer you food, never say "hai"

If you are eating in a Japanese person's home, and they offer you a drink or food, you shouldn't always say "hai." This means yes in English. The most polite way to handle this would be to say, "kekko desu." This means "no, thank you" in the English language. You could also use the phrase "iie, ii desu." This means "No, it's all good" in the English language.

It doesn't matter if you haven't eaten in two days, you must decline the first offer of food or drink to show respect. The second time they offer you drink or food, you can politely accept by saying "ja, itadakimasu, arigatou gozaimasu," which translates to something like: "okay, I will have some, thank you."

If you are dining in a restaurant where you order your drinks and food, it is fine to say "arigatou gozaimasu" to your server to show them that you appreciate their time and service.

- Never put "-san" after your name

We will get into some Japanese honorifics in a little bit, but you need to know that you only use them when you are addressing others. You can't use them after your name.

If you would like to introduce yourself to someone you have just met in Japan, don't say: "Hello, my name is Bobby-san" or "I am Kathy Clubb-san." This is completely wrong. Saying this makes you sound silly and like a child. The right way to say it is: "Hello, my name is Bobby." Or "I'm Kathy Clubb."

- Never address others by using their first name

You never address another person by their first name as we do in the Western world. Japanese people don't think that this is polite, especially if you are talking to somebody who is older than you, or if you have just met someone. You have to use the following honorifics to show them respect:

o "-kun" – this is an informal honorific that is the male form of "-chan." It is normally used for young peers, close male friends, and boys. You could call your friend from school or close coworker, whose name is Kenta "Kenta-kun."

o "-chan" – this is normally used as a female endearment term for close friends, family, and children. Some Japanese will call their grandmother "oba-chan."

o "-san" – this is an honorific that is equal to the "Mr." or "Ms." It can be used to address acquaintances, bosses, coworkers, teachers, and anybody you've just met. If you would like to address someone who has the name of Mr. Kimura, you could just call him "Kimura-san."

o "-sama" – this is the most formal honorific. You would add this to the end of a name to show respect. It is normally used for God or royalty. For God, it would be "kami-sama," while for royalty, it would be "ohime-sama."

Of all these honorifics, "-san" would be the best one when you are addressing any Japanese person. If your tour guide introduces themselves as "Hanako," you could call them "Hanako-san."

Chapter 13

COMMON JAPANESE EXPRESSIONS

You have decided to travel to Japan, but you don't know how to speak Japanese. Not to worry, here is a list of simple phrases that will get you through. If you don't have much time to learn Japanese properly, and you don't have somebody to help you, you just need to read on to learn these easy phrases. Hopefully, you will be able to use most of these when traveling through Japan.

1. "I don't feel well.",
   ぐあいがわるいです、 guai ga warui desu

   Guai simply means a condition. Warui simply means bad. Put them together, guai ga warui desu is just the formal way to tell someone that you aren't feeling well or that you are ill. If you

195

would like to be more specific about where the problem might be, it might sound something like this. "Onaka no guai ga warui desu" or ぐあいがわるいです. This is what you tell somebody that your stomach doesn't feel well.

2. "One more time." もういっかい, mou ikkai

    Mou simply means more, and ikkai simply means one time. So when you put them together, you get mou ikkai, which is an informal way of asking for something again. The formal version of this is: "mou ikkai onegaishimasu" or もういっかいおねがいします

3. "This is interesting/fun." おもしろいです, omoshiroi desu

    Omoshiroi simply means interesting or fun. The polite way to say that something is interesting is omoshiroi desu. The polite way to say that something isn't interesting is: "omoshiroku nai desu" or おもしろくないです

4. "I'm fine now." **だいじょうぶです**, daijyoubu desu

Daijyoubu simply means you're fine, or it's okay. The polite way to say "no" or when you are declining an offer is daijyoubu desu. You could say this when your server is offering more food, water, tea, etc.

5. "I like this/you/it.", **すきです**, suki desu

Suki simply means to like. When you use the phrase "suki desu," you are telling them something you like without having to say what you are admiring. This will come in handy if you don't know the best word for something. If you are certain of the word for something, you could say: "(object's name) ga suki desu." If there is a time when you don't like a certain thing, you would say: "suki janai desu." This is a polite way of letting a person know you don't like something.

6. "Do you have Wi-Fi?" Wi-Fiありますか? Wi-Fi arimasuka?

   This way, you will be able to connect with the internet. You can ask anybody in a café, restaurant, or shop this phrase. If they have free Wi-Fi, they will give you the password. Many Tokyo train stations will have free Wi-Fi. Arimasuka simply means, "Do you have?" This phrase can be used, and you can add in whatever object you might need like toilet paper, shampoo, toothpaste, etc.

7. "How much is it?" いくらですか? ikura desuka?

   Ikura simply means "how much?" Ikura desuka can be used if you aren't sure of the name of something. If you know the product's name, you would ask: "(product name) wa ikura desuka?"

8. "May I have...?" ーをください, ... wo kudasai

Wo is a conjunction, and kudasai is a nice way to say please. When you use this phrase, you will be able to look at anything up close. It could mean you would like to buy a certain product.

9. "Go straight." まっすぐです, massugu desu

A simple definition of massugu is straight. This makes massugu desu the polite way of asking someone to go straight. When you replace massugu with a direction like left, right, down, or up, you will be able to give directions politely.

10. "Left, right, down, or up" ひだり、みぎ、した、うえ, hidari, migi, shita, ue

These are very basic words, and I'm not sure that you would ever use them, but they might come in handy if you are trying to tell someone which way they need to go.

11. "Where is...?" ーわどこですか？, ... wa doko desuka?

Doko simply means where. Desuka is the way to end a sentence when asking a question. The formal way to ask directions is by saying dokodesuka. The informal way to ask directions is doko. You can use this phrase to ask directions.

12. "I want to go to...", ーえいきたいです, ... e ikitai desu.

Ikitai simply means "I want to go." You would use this phrase if you hailed a cab and need to let them know where you are going. Taxi is "takushi" or たくし.

13. "This is my...", わたしの〜です, watashi no ~desu

This is the best way to introduce your traveling companion, friends, or family. To introduce family members in Japanese, you can use these words: relatives or relative, しんせき

(shinseki); parents, **おや** (oya); children or child, **こども** (kodomo); husband, **いっち** (otto); wife, **つま** (tsuma). For different relationships, you can use girlfriend, **かのじょ** (kanojyo); boyfriend, **かれし** (kareshi); friend, **ともだち** (tomodachi).

14. "My name is...", **わたしのなまえわ～です**, watashi no namae wa ～ desu.

Watashi simply means "I." Wa and no are only conjuctions. I'm sure you've figured out by now that namae stands for name, and desu is a normal way to end a sentence in Japanese. When stating a name in Japanese, you always say the last name first, and then you will say the first name. This is the complete opposite of the English language.

15. "Please," **よろしくお願いします**, yoroshiku onegaishimasu

Yoroshiku onegaishimasu could mean several different things. It is mostly used as the formal way to say please. The informal way to say please is yoroshiku.

16. "Thank you," **ありがとうございます**, arigatou gozaimasu

When you need to say thank you in a formal or polite setting, this is what you would use. The informal is simply arigatou. Many people will bow when they say this phrase, and this shows gratitude.

17. "Goodnight," **おやすみなさい**, oyasuminasai

Oyasuminasai is the formal way to tell someone good night. An informal way would be oyasumi. When just learning Japanese, the best way to go is to use the formal.

18. "Good evening," **こんばんわ**, konbanwa

Konbanwa is both an informal and formal way to say good evening. This phrase can be applied when it is night time and when the sun is going down.

19. "Hello," こんいちわ, konnichiwa

Just like konbanwa, konninchiwa is both an informal and formal way to say hello. You can use it in the afternoon, noon, or morning. It is a broad greeting, and mastering it would be very useful.

20. "Good morning," おはようございます, ohayou gozaimasu

You can say good morning, either the informal or formal way. The formal way would be ohayou gozaimasu. If you are greeting new people, stick to the formal way. Ohayou is the informal way.

Chapter 14

SOUND FLUENT WHEN YOU'RE NOT

Let's learn the five most used phrases that are going to make you sound like you have been speaking Japanese since you began talking.

1. "Roger," 了解です, ryokai desu
2. "Speaking of which," そういえば, so ieba
3. "In the meantime," とりあえず, toriaezu
4. "Halfheartedly," 適当に, tekito ni
5. "True," 確かに, tashika ni

CONCLUSION

日本語学習おめでとうございます

Learning Japanese can be tough, but it's a beautiful and rewarding language, rich in history.

We've covered the foundations for learning Japanese, and while you probably still have to practice and learn as you go, you should no longer be stressed about where to start and what to do.

If you're going on vacation to Japan in the next few months, don't stress yourself out about being fluent, simply learn the most common words and phrases you'll need to be able to get around. If your trip is further into the future, you can gain even more.

Remember the things we have gone over, the hiragana and the katakana are basically one and the same. Every sound in Japanese has a character in both alphabets, and it is perfectly okay to stick with the hiragana at first since the characters are more straightforward.

The next step is to start practicing what you just learned. Write out your own kana, or set up your computer so that you can type things in Japanese. As always, say things out loud. Mentioning them in your head is one thing, but once you start hearing yourself saying the words, your brain will begin to absorb them more thoroughly.

Printed in Great Britain
by Amazon

33879734R00122